COWBOY IN CARACAS

*A North American's Memoir of
Venezuela's Democratic Revolution*

by
Charles Hardy

Preface by James W. Russell

Curbstone Press

First Edition: 2007
Copyright © 2007 by Charles Hardy
Preface copyright © 2007 by James W. Russell
ALL RIGHTS RESERVED

Printed in Canada on acid-free paper
cover design: Stone Graphics
cover photographs: top photograph © Jess Hurd/reportdigital.co.uk;
bottom photograph by Johannes Martin

This book was published with the support of
the Connecticut Commission on Culture and
Tourism, and donations from many
individuals. We are very grateful for this
support.

Library of Congress Cataloging-in-Publication Data

Hardy, Charles, 1939-
    Cowboy in Caracas : a North American's memoir of Venezuela's
Democratic revolution / by Charles Hardy. — 1st ed.
        p. cm.
    ISBN-13: 978-1-931896-37-5 (pbk. : alk. paper)
    ISBN-10: 1-931896-37-2 (pbk. : alk. paper)
    1. Venezuela—History—1974-1999—Anecdotes. 2. Caracas
(Venezuela)—Anecdotes. I. Title.

F2328.H37 2007
987.06'33—dc22

                                        2006028805

published by
CURBSTONE PRESS 321 Jackson St. Willimantic, CT 06226
    phone: 860-423-5110   e-mail: info@curbstone.org
                www.curbstone.org

Dedication

To the Dominican Sisters of Sinsinawa, Wisconsin, who taught me how to write and how to think. To my Austrian father, who helped me with my spelling even though he spoke broken English. To my Austrian mother, who encouraged me to climb mountains although she never had. To my best friend who often said, "Tell me what it was like when ..." To the people of Nueva Tacagua, who took me into their homes and into their hearts.

Contents

Preface

Radical revolutions have marked Latin American history every twenty years exactly since the 1959 Cuban revolution. In 1979 victorious Sandinistas marched into Nicaragua's capital to end the notoriously corrupt Somoza dynasty—which Henry Kissinger, surely no friend of leftist revolutionaries, admitted amounted to a kleptocracy. And in 1999 Hugo Chávez became president of Venezuela.

Few would have predicted that Venezuela would move into the vanguard of Latin American revolutionary change. In the 1970s it was by conventional indicators the region's most economically prosperous and politically stable country. It was among the world's leading exporters of oil, and oil was black gold by the end of that decade. It had center-right and center-left political parties that alternated in governing power after nominally democratic elections, much as in the United States.

The images, however, of Venezuela's oil-based prosperity and democratic stability were mirages. There was prosperity and democratic participation but only for a privileged minority who took regular shopping trips to Miami. The majority remained frozen out and living in squalor.

Caracas, the capital city, dramatically illustrated the extremes. It had neighborhoods that were rich by anyone's standards and shopping malls as upscale as any in the world. But ringing them were steep mountainsides to which clung perilously the barrios of the poor. About them Ali Primera wrote one of Latin America's most famous protest songs, "Roofs of Cardboard," describing hovels literally built from cardboard in which thousands of persons lived, many of whom came down each day to work in the kitchens, houses, factories, and malls of the rich.

In 1989 the class tensions of Caracas exploded. The International Monetary Fund pressured the government of President Carlos Andrés Pérez to raise the price of domestic gasoline. That triggered sharp rises in the price of bus tickets, the final straw for people living on the economic edge. They rioted. Pérez called in the army to put them down. Anywhere from hundreds to thousands were killed in what Venezuelans call the Caracazo and what international observers called an IMF riot.

The Caracazo began a meltdown of the traditional political establishment. It punctured the chimera of economic prosperity and political stability. In 1992 a young progressive and charismatic officer, Hugo Chávez, led an unsuccessful attempt to overthrow the government. He was jailed, and then released two years later by a new president. Chávez became the hope of the poor, and in 1998 they gave him enough of their votes so that he took office as president in 1999.

The rich hoped that Chávez's popularity would calm the poor and save the system. Chávez, however, had other intentions. He oversaw the writing of a new progressive constitution and then turned his attention to the country's oil wealth. It had never been distributed to the majority. Instead it benefited the managers and employees of the state oil company, Petróleos de Venezuela or PDVSA, and those who were granted its privileged contracts.

The new constitution made it clear that PDVSA would remain the property of the people of Venezuela and not be privatized, as its managers had sought. Then the Chávez government took steps to wrest control of the company from its corrupt managers so that the oil wealth could be put to the service of the country as a whole and particularly to improve the living conditions of the poor.

Reform of PDVSA threatened the country's traditional oligarchy. With the tacit approval, and perhaps more, of the Bush Administration in the United States, it began plotting a coup d'etat.

The coup came on April 11, 2002. High military officials put Chávez under arrest. The U. S. State Department and the *New York Times* applauded the coup. But when the poor heard, they were furious. They poured out of the barrios and surrounded Miraflores, the national palace, to demand Chávez's return. Faced with this massive outpouring of support for Chávez, the military divided and a large segment revolted against the coup leaders. Chávez returned to the presidency on April 14 in the first reversal of a military coup in modern Latin American history.

But Chávez's enemies did not give up. In December of the same year the management of PDVSA and other employers went on strike to bring down the government. Despite doing substantial economic damage, it fizzled out two months later.

The Organization of American States and the Carter Center then negotiated an agreement between both sides, in which there would be a referendum on the presidency in August 2004. Chávez mobilized his substantial support among the poor and others and won the referendum by a healthy margin of 57 to 43 percent.

Through numerous presidential, National Assembly, and referenda elections, the Chávez government has demonstrated that it has the backing of the majority of Venezuelans. That of course does not stop Venezuelan opponents and the United States from denouncing it as undemocratic. Secretary of State Condoleezza Rice floated the tortured formulation that while Chávez was elected democratically, he was not governing democratically.

Venezuelan supporters of the revolution in turn remember the prescient 1819 comment of their national hero and liberator, Simón Bolívar, that "the United States seems to be destined by fate to plague Latin America with misery in the name of freedom." The only updating necessary is that feigned concern for democracy currently provides the rhetorical cover for imperial interventions.

What the Chávez government has done is to redirect the oil wealth into support for social programs in health and education that benefit the majority of the country instead of being used for the development of further private wealth. The existence of access to the oil wealth of course gives the Chávez government tremendous advantages that the Nicaraguan and Cuban revolutions before it did not have. The Venezuelan revolution is thus unique among Latin American revolutions because, though poverty provoked it, it is not poor.

Enter Charles Hardy, a priest from Wyoming who in 1985 moved to Nueva Tacagua, one of Caracas's poorest barrios. From that vantage point he has witnessed the unfolding of the revolution. In the eloquent and moving pages that follow he takes us into the very heart and soul of this revolution. This is not a book about the larger-than-life Chávez. Rather, it is about the people who support him and why they support him. It is about people who are economically poor but rich in so many other ways as they go through lives of constant struggle to survive with dignity.

Much as many decades before, John Reed in *Insurgent Mexico* captured the bonds that existed between Pancho Villa and his peasant followers in the Mexican revolution—bonds that continue to be sung about in cantinas in Chihuahua today—Hardy captures the reasons why the poor have given Chávez their confidence despite a blizzard of opposition from the country's privately-owned media as well as from the great hegemon to the north, the United States.

Perhaps because he had to learn to speak and listen, not only in a foreign language but also to people in circumstances as different as one can imagine from those he ministered to in

Wyoming, Hardy writes directly and to the point. Occasionally he ponders what he sees in parables but parables that will make the reader nod along with the people from Nueva Tacagua.

For an understanding of Venezuela's revolution, you can do no better than to start with this book.

James W. Russell
Willimantic, Connecticut
January 2007

COWBOY IN CARACAS

A Beginning

Venezuela ?

Winter had not yet officially arrived, but for me it was a very bleak day at the end of 1984 when I heard the news. Bill Boteler, Superior General of the Maryknoll Missionaries, had just told me that I had been accepted as an associate Maryknoll priest and that I was being assigned to Venezuela. I had never had a problem with depression, but for several days after that announcement I was definitely down in the dumps.

I had served for nineteen years as a Roman Catholic priest in the Diocese of Cheyenne, Wyoming. Now I was in the process of going to the foreign missions. I had dreams of Central America, Brazil, Africa, or Asia. "Venezuela," he had said. "Venezuela?" I asked myself. I knew nothing about Venezuela. I didn't even realize that Maryknoll had missionaries there. Instantly, I could have mentally drawn a map with all the other countries on the continent, but I wasn't sure where Venezuela was located in South America. I simply had never heard much about Venezuela nor did I have any interest in it.

Johnny Carson and Ed McMahon once joked about my birthplace, Wyoming, asking each other if it really existed. In my memory, their conversation centered on whether or not they had ever met anyone from Wyoming. With a population of less than half a million, native Wyomingites were and are a rare commodity in the world. Carson and McMahon proposed that Wyoming was perhaps just a space on the map that had to be filled in with some name or other, and so a geographer had put "Wyoming" there. I felt the same way about Venezuela.

I left Bill Boteler's office and went to the library. There I discovered that Venezuela had natural resources and ranching. Oil and cattle. It sounded like Wyoming. I was leaving my home state and the people I loved to simply go to another Wyoming? It didn't make sense, and my enthusiasm dwindled.

I had been fascinated with Maryknoll since elementary school. Their magazine, *The Field Afar,* stirred exciting images in my mind when I was a child. As an adult, I was inspired with their commitment to the oppressed throughout the world.

I knew that in some circles the Maryknoll missionary organization had a reputation for being a rather liberal group. In the months I spent at their headquarters in Ossining, New York, I quickly discovered that such an opinion was a great simplification. I found that some in Maryknoll were to the right of Attila the Hun. Others were to the left of Che Guevara. And some who were at one extreme on religious issues were at the other extreme on social and political issues, and vice versa. Most were somewhere in the middle. What seemed to me to characterize all was a concern to serve the oppressed, something I respected, admired, and wanted to imitate.

That's why my assignment threw me. Oppressed people in Wyoming? Or, should I say, Venezuela?

I was to have a furlough in Wyoming for Christmas and then leave for South America immediately after New Year's Day, 1985. While in my hometown of Cheyenne, I visited one day with Margaret Laybourn. Her mother, Mrs. Reed, had once lived across the street from my family. She got *The New York Times* on Sundays and would often pass it on to us. That might not sound like much, but in Cheyenne, Wyoming, it wasn't your ordinary household that received *The New York Times.*[1] Her daughter did not turn out to be ordinary either.

I think Margaret was Cheyenne's first antiwar protester. The Atlas missiles were to be headquartered at the F. E. Warren Air Force Base that abuts the western city limits. The day the dedication ceremonies were to be held, a very pregnant Margaret took two of her children and a third in a stroller and stood at the entrance of the dedication building

4

with a sign that read, "Mankind must put an end to war or war will put an end to mankind." As a result, the attending generals, senators, and other dignitaries had to enter the building by a back door although everyone saw Margaret and the sign she had printed with shoe polish. It may not have been a great accomplishment for the history books, but it was quite a feat for a petite woman standing alone with three children.

When I told Margaret about my unhappiness with the Venezuelan assignment, she replied, "Maybe it's good that you are going there now while things are calm. Then when things do start to happen, you will have your feet on the ground." Margaret knew more about the world than I did, but I doubt that she realized the full implication of what she was saying.

What I will try to do in the following pages is to give the reader an introduction to the Venezuelan land that my feet trod for the first time in January 1985, and what has happened there since then. It will be an anecdotal history because that is the only way I can think of to give the reader a feel for the Venezuelan reality. But that "feel" comes from having lived for eight years in a pressed-cardboard-and-tin shack in a barrio[2] hidden from the mainstream of Caracas. It was there that I encountered some of the finest people I have ever had the privilege to know.

Reporter friends tell me that it is now recognized that there is no such thing as "objective" journalism. They say the aim today is to give a "balanced" presentation. This book does not give a balanced presentation. I have tried to write it from the viewpoint of the oppressed. It certainly is a biased perspective, but I feel it is an important view of Venezuela that is seldom presented.

It is also different, therefore, from the perspective an international correspondent might have who works in a downtown office building of an opposition newspaper and lives in an apartment in a wealthy neighborhood. I would presume that one day such a person might write a history of this period also. If and when he or she does, I would expect them to acknowledge their bias, something that was never done in their previous reporting about Venezuela.

THE SETTING

Getting My Feet on the Ground

I first visited the barrio Nueva Tacagua in January 1985. It was a government project, constructed on the periphery of Caracas during the first term of President Carlos Andrés Pérez (1974-1979). The barrio was made up of various types of dwellings. There were pressed-cardboard-and-tin shacks in the form of barracks. A panel of cardboard was the only wall separating one home from another. There were apartment buildings, ranging from four to ten stories in height, none with elevators. Some people lived in "trailers" which were similar to metal ship containers and more like ovens when the heat bore down on them. There were also small cinder-block houses.

The barrio was constructed on unstable ground, causing continual landslides that regularly fractured the walls of the more permanent dwellings.

The barracks and trailers were considered "temporary." In reality, all the structures were temporary because of the instability of the land. I often joked about this word "temporary," saying that I had problems understanding Spanish. The structures had been there for over ten years. What did "temporary" mean in Spanish?

After several months of language school in Bolivia and orientation in Venezuela, I was assigned to Nueva Tacagua and offered the possibility of living in one of the cardboard barracks, House Number 51 on Terrace B of Sector C. One day in August of that year, I took a public *Yip*[3] there.

Suitcase in hand, I started to walk toward my future home. Luis, an eight-year-old boy, asked if he could help. I wasn't exactly sure where Number 51 was located, although I had been there before. When we arrived, Luis stopped me from putting my suitcase on the ground, cautioning, "*Caca!*" That's a word Venezuelans use to say "no" to their children. It also means "excrement." Luis was using both meanings of the word.

9

I had just stepped onto a mountain of fecal matter. I don't think there was a square inch of Terrace B that had not been tainted by human or animal excrement at some time. The problem was threefold: lack of running water, lack of toilets, and lack of enclosed sewers. In front of my door, a stream of black water carried the sewage from my neighbors' dwellings to the miniature black river behind my house. Soon I would cease to notice the stench. That day I did.

It would be best to stop and reflect on this situation before going further. Understanding that water and fecal material are essential to understanding Nueva Tacagua.

When Nueva Tacagua was first constructed, there were common toilets that were rendered useless by the lack of water. Because the toilets were of little value and totally unsanitary, the people tore them down and filled the vacant spaces with more shacks.

What does one do to take care of basic necessities when there are no toilets and no open fields? Urinating was no problem. Each home had a corner from which the urine ran below the cardboard wall and into a canal. But to defecate? It was senseless to use something like a potty since there was always a scarcity of water with which to clean it afterwards.

What the inhabitants did was use newspaper. We would squat over the paper, defecate, wrap it up, and throw the newspaper with its contents down the hillside on which the terrace was located, or up the hillside behind my house.

In the morning, when neighbors walked out of their homes with the paper in their hands, no one spoke to each other. It was just a moment of ignominy. No word was adequate for what we felt, and even a "good morning" would have hurt.

The missionaries who lived in Number 51 before me had installed a toilet, the only one I knew of on the terrace. It had no tank. It was simply something to use when there was water. The contents ran a few yards through a shallow underground pipe to the common ditch where it joined the urine of others. But often I did not have enough water to use it.

Water arrived on Terrace B in tank trucks with the words "DRINKING WATER" painted on their sides. They were old and dirty and the hoses that carried the water to our barrels were equally disgusting. We had to pay for each barrel of water. The price was much, much higher than what the wealthy in other parts of town paid for the same quantity, which they received through their faucets.

I originally had two barrels in Number 51 and later bought a third one. We never knew when the trucks would return. Sometimes more than a month passed without water. When it came, clothes were washed, baths were enjoyed, and the mood of the people was different. When it didn't come, children didn't attend school for lack of clean clothes, people tended to stay close to home, and one could feel the tension.

The Venezuelan is an extremely clean person. Body odor is not tolerated. The Venezuelan frequently jokes about the offensive smells of foreigners. I remember a cartoon showing some indigenous people watching the first Europeans stepping onto the shore of their "new world." One says to another: "Do you think they couldn't find any water in the ocean to take a bath with?"

Not having sufficient water and not knowing when it might come again was like torture. One day when a mother had beaten her child, I commented to a neighbor youth that everyone seemed so tense. He replied, "Charlie, have you forgotten that we haven't had water for over a month?"

On one such occasion we went to the press to have our complaint printed. The day following publication of the article the head of the water department issued a statement saying that our complaint was not based on reality. He said that every day he sent two trucks full of water to Terrace B. It was one of my first experiences with how the press was, and still is, used to serve the dominant interests.

Separating my house from my neighbors' was only the

panel of pressed cardboard. We were so close to one another that I probably participated in the lives of about ten families. One morning I stepped out of my house and a neighbor woman asked if I was feeling better. I said, "yes," and thanked her for her concern. Then I asked her how she knew that I had been ill. She replied, "We could tell by the way you've been breathing the past few nights that you weren't well."

Gradually, I became oblivious to the sounds around me, just as I no longer noticed the smells. But I remember kneeling on the floor one evening in front of a termite-eaten crucifix. In the background I heard the words of a song, "Boys just want to have sex. Girls just want to have fun." I wondered if the person playing the music understood the words. Being the only gringo there, I might have been the only person who knew what was being sung. It was a far cry from the Gregorian chant that I had heard for eight years in a seminary many years before.

During the time I was living in Nueva Tacagua I made it a habit to take a day off every week and leave the barrio. While others who worked with us burned out, my respites gave me time for reflection and saved my sanity. My neighbors did not have that luxury. There were also many moments when people lost their sanity.

I could write a whole book about the oppressive situation in Nueva Tacagua, but I hope this gives some idea of life there. Having a feel for barrio life is essential to understanding recent Venezuelan history.

Two Aerial Views of Venezuela

Columbus touched Venezuelan soil in 1498. Spaniards later gave the country the name of Venezuela, or "Little Venice," because the homes of the indigenous people were built on stilts around Lake Maracaibo. Today the country of Venezuela is about six times the size of New York State, occupying 340,600 square miles (912,050 sq. km.) and has a population of about twenty-six million inhabitants, or about one-fourth more than New York.

There was little development during the four hundred years following the arrival of the first Europeans. Then the first oil well gushed in 1922. Today it is no secret that there is oil in Venezuela; it is the world's fifth largest exporter and has the largest reserves of any country. But it has also been blessed with an abundance of natural beauty. There is a tourism poster that describes Venezuela as "the best kept secret of the Caribbean." That may be true.

The northern coast of Venezuela is lined with beautiful beaches. Most of them are separated from the rest of the country by an offshoot of the Andes, which runs east to west along the coast. To get to the beaches one usually has to cross the mountains, many of which contain tropical rain forests. The water of the Caribbean Sea is warm all year long, and the country is fortunate in not being in the hurricane paths that affect much of the area every year. Venezuela also has islands, such as Margarita and Los Roques.

The beaches may attract most of the tourists who visit Venezuela, but the mountains are also spectacular. In the western part of the country, the five peaks surrounding the city of Mérida are higher than any in the United States, except some in Alaska. Even in Alaska there are only four peaks higher than Venezuela's 16,427-foot Pico Bolívar. It is claimed that the world's highest and longest aerial cable cars go to the top of Pico Espejo, which rises 15,633 feet.

In the southeast, the 3,212-foot drop of Angel Falls ranks

it as the highest in the world. The Tepuyes, which abound in the area, are high plains that surge steeply from the ground. An airplane trip is necessary to appreciate their magnificence. Nevertheless, tourism is a largely untapped source of employment and income for the country.

But there are other underestimated opportunities here that the government would like to exploit to move the country away from its dependence on oil. Agriculture is one of them.

I have a sister who is a coffee fanatic. She visited Venezuela in 1992 and tried the most popular brand of coffee in the barrios. It comes in simple plastic wrapping, not at all elegant. My sister, a self-proclaimed coffee connoisseur, thinks it is the best in the world, and for the last ten years has tried to drink nothing else. Could Venezuela someday compete with Colombia and Brazil in the coffee market?

One day in an airport duty-free shop, I picked up a bottle of a French liqueur. On the back I read that the manufacturer had selected some of the world's finest cacao beans from Venezuela.

But the best-kept secret of all would be the ordinary Venezuelan. Within the country, there are a few sayings that might explain this. One of the first things that I heard when I came to the country was, "We Venezuelans are lazy." I would see people waiting for public transportation at five or six in the morning to go to work, and then see them come home, exhausted, at seven or eight at night. But I would still hear them say, "We Venezuelans are lazy."

I gradually discovered that this mind-set was an excellent way to keep a people oppressed. As factory workers and domestic help heard the saying repeated over and over, they began to accept the idea as true even if it wasn't.

The mistreatment of the ordinary Venezuelan would be a valuable study for a social scientist. One day I spoke to a young man who had worked for five years in the same shoe factory. I asked him if he had had any advancement in position or if that possibility existed. The reply was, "No.

The owners are foreigners." I frequently heard of factories that would go out of business in December and start anew in January, to avoid paying social security benefits to long-term employees. Another common saying is, "I'm not stupid. Do you think I'm an Indian?" I recently had a conversation with a Guajiro[4] laborer who had only six grades of formal education. He reads everything he can get his hands on. I was impressed with his knowledge of world geography, among other things. Still, the stereotype of the indigenous person is that of being uneducated.

Most Venezuelans represent a mixture of the blood of the Europeans who came to conquer, the blacks who were brought as slaves, and the indigenous people who have been here for centuries. Nevertheless, those who control commerce are generally of foreign extraction and have light skin—two advantages for success. Racism also lies at the root of Venezuela's current crisis, something I will discuss later.

So, looking out from an airplane, one could easily overlook this treasure that is the ordinary Venezuelan. It is not even recognized by the Venezuelan. But looking within an airplane one day I came to understand another dimension of the misperception of the Venezuelan, the one that many foreigners seem to have.

One day, on an international flight from Caracas, I was talking to a flight attendant about the current situation in Venezuela. She remarked, "You know what another attendant said to me a few moments ago? She said that it had been so long since she had been on the Caracas-U.S. route that she had forgotten how snobbish the wealthy Venezuelan is."

A few months later I checked out her remarks with some flight attendants on another international flight. Their response was similar.

Their remarks brought to mind a visit I had with an executive on the island of Curaçao. He said, "In my opinion,

Venezuelans are the most arrogant people in the world. They not only think they are better than anyone else but they like to show it." I said that had not been my experience, but I had to admit that my experience was limited to barrio dwellers. I have never had much contact with the upper classes.

The executive then went on: "There was one exception. My wife and I were staying at the Caracas Hilton for about a week and we had the same taxi driver each day. After a few days he said to us: 'If you would like to, tomorrow I would like to show you my Venezuela and I won't charge you anything.' He took us to places near Caracas and, most important of all, he took us to his home where his wife prepared a meal for us. It was a wonderful day, and we kept in communication for years until we moved and lost his address."

I said to the man, "That is the Venezuelan that I know."

I think it is important to mention this because during the social conflicts of 2002 I came to be more and more aware of the attitude described by the executive and the flight attendants. There was displayed an attitude of extreme superiority on the part of the wealthy and upper middle class opposition, who used the words "the civil society" in order to distinguish themselves from the supporters of the government, a large number of whom are barrio dwellers and whom they called "the hordes."

To understand the secrets of Venezuela, it is not enough to look out from an airplane. One must look within them, and one must also touch the ground.

A View of Caracas from the Barrio

Caracas is not Venezuela, but it likes to think it is. Its relation to the rest of the country would be similar to that of New York City to the whole United States. Caracas is the center for the principal television channels, radio stations, and daily newspapers. It is home to about one-fourth of Venezuela's twenty-six million inhabitants, many of whom migrated there from the countryside and from other parts of the world. Italians, Portuguese, Spaniards, and Arabs abound, each with their own specialty. The Italians are builders. The Portuguese (most from the island of Madeira) own the bakeries, meat markets, and grocery stores. The Spaniards run hotels and restaurants, and the Arabs sell furniture and any other commodity that might have general appeal.

There are also many immigrants from other Latin American countries, especially Colombia and Ecuador.

Venezuelans, in general, have been the employees, not the employers. And while they also live in Caracas, it is not their native home either. Most seem to have come from the countryside, migrating to Caracas for work and closer proximity to hospitals, schools, and other services.

Every Christmas and Easter there is a massive movement of bodies as Caracas empties. The Venezuelans fill the bus stations and national airport. Those of foreign extraction and the upper classes take over the Simón Bolívar International Airport. It is seen as a penance to be in Caracas at these times, a punishment for those who do not have family elsewhere or lack the money to go visit them.

The importance of Caracas might be highlighted in an event that occurred during the general rioting in February and March of 1989. Radio stations throughout the country always played the national anthem at 6 a.m., noon, and 6 p.m. Other countries might have played the angelus bells at these times, but Venezuela played the national anthem. It is reported that President Andrés Pérez ordered the stations to discontinue the practice not long after the rioting began. The reason? The anthem contains the words, "Follow the example which Caracas has set for us." The words were written in 1810 when the city council of Caracas declared Venezuela's independence from Spain. But with tens of thousands looting in the streets of Caracas the words took on a different meaning. Fourteen years later, the stations still did not play the anthem.

Entering Caracas at night, you have the feeling you are entering a Christmas tree as the lights on the hillside glitter around you. But the daytime reality is different. Someone described Caracas as a bathtub with a dirty ring around it. In contrast to the king who lives in the castle and looks down on his subjects, it is the lower classes who look down on the upper classes in a good part of Caracas.

The barrio structures, which hardly appear beautiful to the unaccustomed eye, are really an architectural wonder. I doubt many architects could accomplish what the ordinary Venezuelan has done. The sweat and labor involved in carrying water, cement, gravel, and all the other necessary materials up the mountains surrounding Caracas would make an army of ants proud of the final product.

This is not to say that the wealthy do not also live on hillsides. However, Spanish has many words for hills. The lower classes, therefore, live in the *cerros*. The wealthy live in the *prados*, the *lomas*, or the *cumbres*. After the rioting in 1989, a book was published titled *The Day the Hills Came Down*. The word used for hills was *cerros*. There was no doubt where the people came from.

Symbols of Revolution

Some years ago a terrible tornado hit Charles City, Iowa. One of my sisters and her husband lived there at the time. A few months later they visited Cheyenne and tried to share their experiences of the event. I could see in the faces of their listeners not only that they didn't understand what my family members were saying, but also that there was little interest in the matter.

One person said, "Yes, I remember when we saw a tornado some miles from our farmhouse." My relatives were not talking about "some miles from." They were talking about "right there."

I have had the same experience whenever I have returned to the United States from Latin America. I say this not to blame us North Americans. It is often simply difficult to understand what one has never experienced. And yet, if we truly want a better world for everyone, we've got to try.

A word that is often associated with Latin America is "revolution." In Venezuela, President Chávez has often spoken of the need for a "peaceful revolution," but that word can quickly provoke fear and misunderstanding.

We U.S. citizens seem to have totally forgotten that our country came into existence because of a revolution and that an item as seemingly insignificant as tea was an important symbol of that revolution. It was never England's intention to sit side by side someday in the United Nations with what was supposed to be a colony. There was a revolution that culminated in a Declaration of Independence. But in the twenty-first century, what was good for the U.S. in the eighteenth century is today a threat in the minds of many people. Maybe it should be. But the memory of the Boston Tea Party might help us to understand what is happening today.

I think it was Sukarno who once said something to this effect: To those who have a refrigerator, a refrigerator is just a refrigerator. To those who have none, it is a symbol of revolution.

The same could be said of many things. In the early sixties, I remember seeing people in Mexico City standing in front of a display window, looking at a television set. It brought to mind the scenes in a Christmas story about a little match girl looking through a store window at the toys she would never have. I sensed fascination in the people standing there. I also sensed something of an impossible dream.

In the 1980s, television sets were common in Nueva Tacagua. Visitors often questioned how it was that the people could afford TV. If they could have seen the second-, third- and fourth-hand sets, the question might not have been asked. But a more relevant question would have been why they had sets. There is not much to do when you are confined in one area and lack transportation. TV gave both children and adults something to do. It was a means of escape from reality.

In Nueva Tacagua the water we mentioned earlier, not television, was probably the most prominent symbol of revolution. Or, shall I say, the lack of water. I hadn't been there long before I realized that two barrels of water could disappear rapidly if one wasn't careful. As a result, people in the apartments washed their dishes in one basin of soapy water, and rinsed them in another basin. When the soapy water became dirty, it became water for the toilets in the apartment buildings, and the rinse water became the soapy water. In that way, each drop of water was used three times. When I bathed, I would use about one gallon of water and would stand in a tub so that the water could be collected and then used to flush the toilet.

One day I went downtown and saw a woman washing her sidewalk with a hose. I approached her and asked her how she could do that when people in the barrios didn't have any water. She just looked at me as if I were from another world. I was. Later on, when McDonald's opened a fast-food restaurant in the Chacaito area of Caracas, it hurt to see their employees hosing down the parking lot.

One evening I had to take someone to the hospital for an emergency. Sitting outside with a couple of neighbors, waiting to hear what was happening to the person, I opened a Christmas card from the United States. There was a letter enclosed in which the writer told me at length about an evening when the water in her neighborhood was shut off for four hours. I laughed as I translated it to the others. When I finished, one of them corrected me: "Charlie, that person took time to write you about something important to her. You shouldn't minimize its importance." I was in the presence of people much holier than I.

I also think they weren't voicing their deeper feelings about water: to those who have water, water is simply water. But to those who don't, it is a symbol of revolution.

But water was only one of a multitude of symbols. Just leaving the barrio was a kind of psychological torture. Imagine a woman leaving the barrio to work in a wealthy person's home as a cook or possibly as a cleaning lady in an office. Venezuelans are very conscious of appearance. A woman might even be wearing high heels. First she climbs up a hillside to the transportation stop and then stands and waits for a *Yip*. When it comes, she has to push to try to be one of the twelve who get a seat. In the back of these Toyota Land Cruisers, she sits on one of the two wood planks covered with a little padding. Exactly five average-sized persons fit on each board. If one is chubby, the rest suffer with him or her. No one wants the middle seats because there is usually a break in the cushions and no padding there. There is also nothing to hold on to. It is simply the pressure of other bodies that keeps you from moving. (If you still cannot imagine the environment, just open a can of sardines and meditate on them.)

When the *Yip* arrives at its destination, she then has to walk a few blocks to a Metro (subway) station. Caracas's

Metro system is comparable to the most modern in the world and extremely clean. No one chews gum, eats, or smokes after entering the stations. There is never a piece of paper on the floor of the stations or within the cars. But there is a difference in the stations. If you are in the western part of the city, home of the barrios of Catia, the walls are neat, clean, and colorful, but made of cinderblock. If you are in the other parts of the city, the walls are covered with ceramic tiles. A subtle symbol, but a symbol nevertheless.

Having arrived at her Metro destination, the woman goes up a modern escalator and passes shops displaying exquisite clothing. Then she boards a modern Metro bus or a smaller privately owned bus to go to her final destination. There, the majority of the people are fair-skinned, except for the laborers, cleaning and cooking personnel, and security guards. The inhabitants have their own automobiles and do not have to use the public transportation systems: another symbol of the reality.

While there, she goes shopping in a modern supermarket for the family she works for. She sees fruit, vegetables, and meat superior to what she could buy in the barrio and at more economical prices. Subconsciously, even fruit, vegetables, and meat become symbols of revolution.

At night, she wearily returns to another reality. After crawling out of the sardine can, she arrives at her shack. An older child, who couldn't attend school that day, took care of her little ones while she was gone. Glancing at the television as she prepares a late supper, she sees the ordinary homes of families in the United States or those of Venezuelans who live in homes similar to the one where she spent her day. Then she tucks her children into bed and prays that the rats will not bite them during the night.

If you can multiply days like this by the hundreds and the symbols by thousands, you will more easily understand what happened in Caracas on February 27, 1989.

THE PLAY

When Things Started Happening

It was in late 1988 that I realized something was going to happen in Venezuela. I had just returned from a furlough in the United States and had received some funds with which the Nueva Tacagua pastoral team decided to buy a Jeep Wrangler. The problem was that there were none available. There were no new vehicles of any kind for sale. The showrooms were empty!

It was election time in Venezuela and the party in power, Acción Democrática, wanted to be sure that they won the elections, so prices were strictly controlled. One dealer finally referred me to an agency that had two Jeeps. I went there and bought one for about five thousand dollars. It seemed to be an excellent deal. Within a few days, I discovered that the odometer cable had been cut. It wasn't a new vehicle after all, but there was nothing I could do about it. A great scandal developed in Venezuela at that time about the use of some Jeeps by the Lusinchi government during the election campaign. I think I bought one of them.

But buying a car wasn't the ordinary Venezuelan's main concern. There were shortages of rice, corn flour, black beans, and other commodities that make up the basic Venezuelan diet. Just as the car dealers and manufacturers were holding back their products waiting for the prices to go up again, so were the owners of grocery stores and supermarkets.

In January and February of 1989, one could feel the tension rising. I remember standing in line to use a public telephone when a heated discussion erupted over some insignificant matter.

The price of bread went from three pieces for one bolívar to one piece for two bolívars in a matter of a few weeks, an increase of about six hundred percent. I have often asked U.S. citizens to think about how they would react if the price of a loaf of bread suddenly went from two dollars to twelve dollars.

On February 2, 1989, Carlos Andrés Pérez assumed the presidency. Many saw it as a coronation ceremony because of its extravagance. Dignitaries from throughout the world were present. The vice-president of the United States, Dan Quayle, was sitting in the same row as Fidel Castro.

In his inaugural address, Pérez spoke a lot about world diplomacy and hardly referred to the problems within the country. Lusinchi had left very little money in the nation's treasury. A famous Venezuelan, José Ignacio Cabrujas, wrote that Pérez was expected to be a magician. His job was not to pull just one magic rabbit out of a hat but a multitude of rabbits that would change the course of the economy.[5]

During his first term as president, there was an abundance of money from oil. Everyone had a job. That did not mean that everyone had work, however. Aristóbulo Istúriz did not belong to either of the two major parties. When he was unexpectedly elected mayor of the Libertador district of Caracas in 1993, it is said he discovered that there were about eighty doorkeepers for the city hall. There was only one entrance and only one or two doorkeepers on duty at any moment, but every two weeks eighty doorkeepers showed up for their pay.

When I shared this story with a health insurance salesman, he asked if I remembered the situation in the Pérez Careño Hospital where there were sixty ambulance drivers for one ambulance. Then he added, "But the worst thing about it was that the ambulance had been out of service for years, in need of repairs!"

But now the financial situation of the country was different. On February 16, Pérez announced his new economic policies and on Sunday, February 26, the price of gasoline went up.

Then, the morning of February 27, Caracas exploded. It seems to have started in a suburb of the city as people began boarding buses to go to work. The drivers had raised their fares because the price of gasoline had increased the day before. They had not been officially authorized to do so, but they said they could not wait.

There had been no leaders, no planning, and no organization. But within hours tens of thousands of people were in the streets, and looting began. First it was food, then clothing, then anything one could get. There are photos of people carrying televisions and even refrigerators.

Not all stores were looted. In one barrio, a newspaper reporter noted that the local hardware store was left untouched. The neighbors said that the owner was a Venezuelan who always charged low prices and even sold on credit.

The reaction of the police was interesting. Many, being underpaid and from the poorer classes, identified with those who were looting. I spoke to one policeman afterwards who said he fired only one shot during those days of looting. He was trying to maintain order outside a supermarket, insisting that the people stay in line to enter and do their looting. A woman approached him and reprimanded him for not stopping the people. He replied that he was doing what he could to preserve lives. "Then I'm going in too!" she said. He pulled out his revolver, shot it into the air, and answered her, "No way! Get out of here."

As the day went on, the attitude of the police changed. They too became looters. Reporters saw them firing tear gas to scare others away from stores. Then they entered and filled their police vehicles with merchandise.

They also became assassins, firing indiscriminately into crowds running away from them. The looters discovered the rice, beans, cornmeal, etc., which had not been available for weeks, hidden in storerooms. Stealing spaghetti suddenly merited the death penalty. The situation became worse when the president ordered the army into the streets.

In a newspaper interview some months before, I had said

that I had been taught in moral theology classes that if someone has no food, it is not stealing if he takes some from someone who has too much. My words had no effect on what was happening, though it was good moral theology in practice. Nevertheless, I hoped no official would recall my words.

But it wasn't only looters who were killed. In Nueva Tacagua a young man left his home dressed in shorts and a t-shirt to visit his girlfriend a few houses away. There were no places to loot in that area, but he was killed.

In another part of Caracas, a father left home to go to work at 5:50 a.m., ten minutes before the curfew was to end. He was shot dead. Another father was killed in bed with his child in his arms as a stray bullet entered the apartment.

Stories also abounded of street people who were eliminated.

In one barrio, a dog barked at a soldier. The soldier shot her. The young master of the dog protested. He, too, was shot. The master died. The dog survived and later gave birth to pups. I know this story because my family became the owner of one of the pups.

No one knows the number of deaths that occurred in Venezuela during the tumultuous days of February and March, 1989. I would not be surprised if the number surpassed that of the massacre in Tianamen Square in China three months later. The China event received extensive press coverage, and the date is still remembered every year. But what happened in Caracas received little coverage and was quickly forgotten.

Numbers at such moments get elevated or diminished, depending on their political value. *The World Almanac and Book of Facts 1993*[6] spoke of an estimated five thousand who died and ten thousand who were injured in Tianamen. There was no mention of the deaths in Venezuela. Three years later, the *1996 Information Please Almanac*[7] mentioned only "several hundred deaths" in China and, again, said nothing about those in Venezuela.

Originally, there were rumors of thousands dead in the streets, information that was relayed by people in positions of responsibility. The Venezuelan government said that there were 276 deaths. But by 1990, human rights groups were able to give the names and identity numbers of 399 people who had died, and even that was an incomplete listing.

That many people disappeared was a reality, but a reality that the government denied. There were rumors of secret burial places, but it wasn't until November, 1990, that a judge had enough information to order the excavation of some ground in an isolated part of the West Cemetery of Caracas in an area called La Nueva Peste, "The New Plague." There, sixty-eight bodies were discovered in plastic garbage bags. Medical experts were able to identify three of the cadavers as those of youths who had disappeared during the February-March days of 1989. Then the identification process stopped.

While the unearthing of the bodies proceeded, volunteers were asked to be present twenty-four hours a day so that the government could not damage the site. One day two teenage girls appeared at the cemetery. They had seen on television what was happening there. That day, they had skipped school and were carrying a photo of their brother who had disappeared. Their mother had told them never to speak of him again in order to avoid problems for the family. They had disobeyed their mother's instructions.

How many other families carried the same burden as this one? Were there other such sites elsewhere in the cemetery? Elsewhere in the country?

For months afterwards, any small explosion, such as a large firecracker, would set people running. Some shopkeepers closed their doors and moved back to their native countries. Most opened again, but the country was not the same.

Thousands of people had lost family members. Every barrio of Caracas had felt the repression of the police and armed forces. Many of those living in the wealthier parts of the city had their business establishments destroyed, but the deaths they witnessed were mostly on television, and they cheered the police who were chasing the barrio dwellers.

The economic injustices and racial divisions that had existed for years in Caracas and in Venezuela as a whole had surfaced. Ten years later, political opponents of President Hugo Chávez would accuse him of dividing the country. But in 1989 Chávez was just another soldier. Like many Venezuelans, he probably wondered why soldiers should kill hungry people for stealing spaghetti.

Sleeping in the Cemetery

The excavation of the pit where the bodies had been buried in garbage bags began before the Christmas holiday season in 1990. I had the privilege of spending several nights there with some youth from Nueva Tacagua.

At that time of the year, there is a somewhat strange symbol that overlooks the city of Caracas. It is "the Cross of Christmas," a huge illuminated structure located high on the mountains that surround the city. The normal symbol of the Nativity is the star of Bethlehem, not the cross of Jerusalem.

The cross was not visible from where we lived in Nueva Tacagua, but from the cemetery it was easily seen. During that December and the months that followed, the cross seemed extremely appropriate and provided a source for reflection.

The long nights in the cemetery also provided time to share personal stories and memories of what had happened almost two years before. The following are mine.

* * * * *

On Sunday, February 26, 1989, I filled the Jeep Wrangler with gasoline. Following the new government's economic policies, the price was higher than the day before. I sensed a lot of anxiety in my neighbors. I, too, was tense and afraid that something was going to happen. I decided that I definitely would take Thursday off that week and go to the beach.

On the morning of February 27, 1989, I left the barrio to buy a swimsuit. Did I need a new one? No, but I wanted one. I had heard that when one was a bit down in the dumps it was good to do something nice for oneself to pick up one's spirits. As I already mentioned, going to the beach was one way of escaping the tension of barrio life. A new swimsuit seemed like the ticket that would ensure my reservation for a day off.

Little did I know at that moment that by Thursday no one would be at the beach, that the city would have been occupied by federal troops, and that I would have spent a night sleeping on the bare floor of a hospital hallway.

When I stepped out of the La Hoyada subway station that morning, there was a strange feeling in the air. People seemed jittery. I walked a couple of blocks and the clothing store where I was going to shop was closed. Other stores were lowering and raising their santamarias (Holy Marys). That's the word used in Venezuela for the iron gratings or corrugated steel curtains that commercial shops lower over their show windows at night for protection. But it wasn't night. It was midmorning.

I asked a woman standing in front of a partially opened store what was happening. She replied, "I don't know, but *mosca!*" *Mosca* is the word for a "fly" in Spanish. Before that day I hadn't paid any attention to such an expression but from the tone of her voice I knew immediately it also meant "be careful!"

I decided to head back to the subway. Along the way I saw some people running through the streets. I also saw a bus on fire. After retrieving the Jeep that we had just bought, while driving back to the barrio I saw people burning garbage in the streets. As I approached Nueva Tacagua, I began to hear sirens and shots. People were walking down the mountainside to the barrio, since there was no transportation. Most people had walked miles to get home that afternoon. I stopped to look down at the barrio, and I could see smoke billowing up.

Neighbors had set up a barricade of burning tires and rubbish, blocking the principal entrance to the barrio. Self-appointed "guards" were letting only neighbors pass. The blockade appeared to be a somewhat meaningless act, since the only people who ever went to Nueva Tacagua were neighbors or friends. It was a dead end that no one visited by accident.

As I too stood alongside the burning rubbish late into the night, someone said to me, "This doesn't make any sense." They were wrong. It was a chance for the people to ventilate some of their frustration. Would it put rice, black beans, or meat on their tables? No. But screaming together can be therapeutic.

When I went home, I started a letter to members of my family. I had the feeling that it might be my last letter. Tiredness set in and I never finished it.

Tuesday morning the situation was relatively calm in the part of the barrio where I lived. Looting continued in the city, but Nueva Tacagua had been constructed to be isolated from Caracas. Without public transportation, most people were incarcerated within the confines of the barrio, and there wasn't much worth looting in Nueva Tacagua. One of the larger grocery stores was threatened. The owner simply opened the door and said that those who wanted to loot should enter, but asked that they not destroy anything. Only a few entered. The other neighbors just looked on.

However, looking across the ravine that separated Sector C, where I lived, from Sector A-B, one could see a person lying in the middle of a road. The young woman had been shot Monday evening and people were afraid to move the body until the coroner came. He never came and eventually the neighbors painted a white outline around her body on the pavement (just as they had seen police do in movies) and removed her body for burial. How her death occurred was never explained.

I spent the day walking around the barrio, talking to people. A curfew had been decreed, but we had seen no police in Nueva Tacagua since Monday afternoon, so it wasn't taken too seriously.

By Wednesday, I was feeling claustrophobic. Tony, a neighbor youth and catechist, had an eye infection. We decided to see if we could find a doctor to examine it. I was also aware that no one connected with Maryknoll knew whether I was dead or alive since we had no telephones in Nueva Tacagua.

As we drove through the streets, Caracas appeared to be a war zone and a cemetery. Skeletons of stores surrounded us. The sidewalks were covered with shattered glass. The store windows were empty. The military seemed to be everywhere.

But driving into a wealthier part of Caracas to find a clinic, the atmosphere was different. The stores had not been touched. The people had not been physically affected. As is the custom in Caracas neighborhoods, we even found a truck with its owner calmly selling watermelons. It was as though the downtown and the barrios were different worlds from that of the rich.

When we returned to the barrio, everything had changed. At the entrance of Terrace B, where I lived, there was a huge truck filled with soldiers. As they looked down on us with their automatic weapons in their hands, I froze. One motioned us on and I drove to my shack. By the time we got there, the sounds of weapons could be heard.

Surprisingly, the people did not stay in their homes but came out into the street. The cardboard walls would have provided no protection anyway and being with neighbors made one feel better, more secure. Tony said to me, "Charlie, everyone is scared. Do whatever you can to help them." I had no idea what to do in such a situation, so I just walked among them, trying to find something to say.

From Terrace B we could look down on the whole barrio that lay below us. More military trucks were entering. Shots were being fired into the air. Knowing nothing about the range of bullets, each time I heard the sound of shooting I would duck back, away from the edge of the mountainside.

Then someone said, "Did you see that?" I had. The soldiers had shot a man and they were throwing his body down the mountain. It was like a war movie, a horror show.

As I walked along the edge of the terrace, I came upon a

soldier with his automatic weapon. No one was near him. I raised my arms into the air and said, "My name is Charlie. I am the priest here. The people here are good people." I asked him if he was from a barrio, and he replied that he was from the countryside and had been called into action the day before.

I could see tears in his eyes as he looked at us. My neighbors began to gather behind me. I felt sorry for the young man and could imagine how a youth from Cheyenne, Wyoming, would feel if he were suddenly dropped into the slums of a major U.S. city, alone, having been told that it was one of the city's most dangerous areas.

Here he was, faced with men, women, and children who probably looked like his own family. But I also knew that if someone threw a rock, he had the power to kill us all.

A lay missionary later wrote to a priest in the United States that she didn't think I was ever more a priest than that day when I stood between the automatic weapon and the people of the barrio.

Constitutional rights had already been suspended and at six o'clock a curfew was to begin. A neighbor's message was short and to the point: "Charlie, go to your house and don't come out no matter what happens. They will kill you if you do!" I said good evening to everyone and went home.

You have a strange feeling when you live in a cardboard shack. You are as close to the storybook figure of the first of the three little pigs in its house of straw as a human can be. As I listened to the continuing fire from automatic weapons, I knew there was no place to hide. I put water in a pot to boil for some spaghetti, and I knelt to pray.

Before the water was ready, there was a knock at my door. A woman was shouting, "Charlie, Charlie." Fearfully, I opened the door and told her to enter immediately. "Charlie," she said, "my sister is dying. Please take her to the hospital."

My neighbor's earlier warning was still ringing in my ears: "Don't come out. They will kill you." I looked at the woman and said, "Virginia, I don't think I can get your sister to the hospital alive. I am a man. You are a woman. I don't think they will fire at you. Try to find a soldier and tell him about your sister. They are the only ones who can save her." Following my advice she left to look for a soldier.

It was not long before she returned. "There are no soldiers," she said. For some reason, after scaring us, the army had pulled out. Where they were, we didn't know, but they were not in our barrio.

Hearing Virginia's cries, neighbors began to look out of their doors. Tony shouted, "If you go to the hospital, Charlie, I'll go with you." His mother pleaded with him not to go. He ran across the street and told me to dress like a priest, something I seldom did. Levis and a short-sleeved shirt were my usual attire.

I put on a light-blue clerical shirt. Tony said that wouldn't do. "Dress," he said, "the same way you do for Mass." I put an alb and stole over my shirt and Levis. In many ways the garb was appropriate. I was participating in the most profound liturgical celebration of my life, a Mass of the common people.

Meanwhile Tony tore a pillowcase in half and taped it to a broomstick, making it into a white flag.

Virginia's sister was diabetic and had gone into shock when she saw the soldiers throw the man down the mountainside. She lived near that place and had simply been visiting Virginia. Her jaws were locked and she couldn't speak. Neighbors helped her into the back of the Jeep.

It was beginning to get dark. As we drove away, children were shouting, "Chau, Charlie, chau." The name "Charlie" seemed to have fascinated the little children. But that night it wasn't the happy greeting that they usually gave me when I walked into the neighborhood and they chanted, "Charlie, Charlie, Charlie."

Tony turned his head away. Would we ever be back? Would he ever see his mother again?

The Jeep was blue, the same color the police used. If people were shooting at the police, we were targets. On the other hand, we were not police, and since no one who was not an authority was supposed to be on the streets, we were targets for the police and soldiers.

For more than half an hour we drove through the barrios of Catia until we reached the Magallanes Public Hospital. There were no police or soldiers in sight until we arrived there. I took off my church robes, but someone recognized me and said, "Come." He led me through the halls of the hospital to the morgue. Opening the door, I saw three naked dead bodies on tables. Five more were lying on the floor. They were all young people. What I prayed at that moment, I don't remember. I just remember turning my head and hitting it against the wall. I was in a human slaughterhouse.

We spent the evening talking and listening to the firing of automatic weapons. Tony and I had not eaten since breakfast. Some hospital workers gave us the food they had left over from their supper. I ate about nineteen black beans, one at a time. Eventually, with Virginia and the other members of her family who had accompanied us, we all lay down on a cold hallway floor and tried to sleep until 6 a.m. when the curfew would be over and we could leave the hospital.

When six o'clock came, we headed back to the barrio. It was now Thursday, the day I had planned to go to the beach. I didn't go.

From that moment on, the days were tolerable. The nights were long, and as shots rang out one wondered if another naked body would soon be lying on the floor of the hospital morgue.

The Fermentation after the Trampling of Grapes

There is a saying attributed to Simón Bolívar: "Damned be the soldier who uses his weapons against his own people." Yet that was the burden that had been laid upon the shoulders of the armed forces in those February-March days. Within weeks following the 1989 massacre, a group of military officers who had been meeting in secret began discussing what had happened and reflecting on what Bolívar had said. One of them was a young major, Hugo Chávez Frías.

By the end of 1991, the situation in Venezuela had not changed much. The government had not taken into account the suffering of the people, and the protests continued. Almost daily, there were demonstrations against the government and a heavy-handed squashing of them.

The Maryknoll missionaries had their principal offices about a block from the Pedagógico, the Caracas teachers' college. Being U.S. citizens, we used to celebrate Thanksgiving Day even though it is not celebrated in Venezuela. I remember going out one November morning to buy some crepe paper for decorations. The police had blockaded the street that ran in front of the college. They were armed, lined up across the street and facing the college. I had a strange feeling as I crossed behind them that day, wondering if I should or shouldn't.

Each time I had picked up the morning newspaper that November, I expected to read about the death of another student. The PROVEA[8] report for that year provides the following information:

October 30, 1991. Raúl Contreras, age 18, was killed during a student demonstration in Los Teques[9] by an automatic weapon used by a police agent.

November 20,1991. Jarwin Duncan Capoter, age 16, José G. Delgado, age 17, Humberto J. López, age 21, were all executed during the repression of a student demonstration in Caracas by members of the Metropolitan Police.

November 21. 1991. Ricardo Silva, age 16, died in the hospital in Valencia[10] after being wounded by a police agent during a student demonstration.

November 28, 1991. Héctor José Guzman, age 23, died after being wounded by a member of the DISIP (a police group) during the repression of a student demonstration.

Near the teachers' college, graffiti on the wall next to a bakery read, "IF WE ARE THE FUTURE OF THE WORLD, WHY ARE YOU KILLING US?"

Almost three years after the rioting, which was centered in Caracas, the repression continued. I had heard rumors that there would be a serious attempt to overthrow the government of Carlos Andrés Pérez. I had no reason to doubt them. It was just a question of when it would happen.

On the night of February 3, 1992, six family members and friends arrived from the United States. The airport that serves Caracas is on the coast, and one has to drive up the mountain into the city. I noticed more military than usual along the highway but paid little attention to it.

After arriving at the Maryknoll center's house, we talked into the early morning. Before going to sleep we heard some small explosive sounds, but I told my guests that Venezuelans often celebrated birthdays with fireworks, and we went to bed.

When I awoke around 5 a.m., I realized that I was not hearing fireworks but the firing of automatic weapons. Looking out the window I could see the reflection of that on the windows of the surrounding buildings. An attempted coup was underway.

On the twelfth story of an apartment building we seemed safe. We immediately called the U.S. to inform the families of my guests that they had arrived and were ok, just in case communication should be cut off later.

The coup attempt was short-lived. By midday it was over. The government permitted the leader, Lieutenant Colonel Hugo Chávez Frías, to appear on television to tell his followers to put down their arms. He spoke for less than two minutes, but in that time he accepted responsibility for the failure of the attempt and he said that, *por ahora* (for now), the objectives were not attainable.

Had presidential elections been held that day, I believe he would have easily won. One barrio woman said that it was the first time in her memory that she had heard someone in Venezuela accepting responsibility for a failure. In the congress, one person shouted, "Death to the traitors." However, Rafael Caldera, a more levelheaded ex-president, said that the government should recognize that there were serious problems in the country. Caldera would later be elected president; the other man disappeared from political life.

Within days, the walls of the city were covered with the words *POR AHORA*. Chávez and his followers were jailed.

Later, when Chávez became a presidential candidate in the campaign of 1998, the opposition tried to confuse the events of the 1989 massacre with those of the 1992 attempted coup. The idea was to make people think that hundreds, even thousands, had died in the coup of 1992.

According to the research I have been able to do, there were probably about a dozen deaths. The PROVEA report for 1992 says that there were rumors of about eighty deaths, but a check of the hospitals of Caracas showed that only forty-seven deaths were registered that day from all causes.[11] Their report lists the names of only three soldiers, all of whom seem to have been executed by the government after they surrendered. The February 5 issue of the daily newspaper *El Nacional* had the government officially recognizing fourteen deaths. It would have been to the advantage of the government to exaggerate the number of deaths, so this number may be high.

In addition, the deaths of four students in Valencia, which is about two-and-a-half hours from Caracas, should be mentioned. In one case, on February 4, police agents took a young woman off a bus carrying rebel forces and assassinated her. The other three were shot at close range in other circumstances.

It should be noted that the rebellion had the backing not only of the military but also of civilians. This was the beginning of a strange alliance between members of the military and young people involved in student organizations and community action. The military in Latin American countries does not inspire much trust within such circles and has generally been repressive and feared by such groups. Something was happening.

Following the attempted coup, the repression continued. People began beating on pots and pans as a sign of protest. Then there was the night of blowing whistles. There were also statistics. For example, on the night of March 10, 1992, the police killed eight people. Here's the description of what happened in one of the cases during the beating on pans: "Various (police) agents passed by, shooting at a group of youths, among whom was the victim." His age: 15. On April 8, three more teenagers were killed during the whistle blowing, and two men who were wounded died during the following days. The ages of the victims in the assassinations: 24, 16, 16, 17, 18, 31, 19, 18, 15, 40, 35, 16, etc.

As the year was drawing to a close, there was to be a full marathon in Caracas. Some years earlier I had participated in one, and I ran the 26.2 miles with three youths from our barrio and a fellow lay missionary. (I should say, I *survived* one.) I decided that I would like to try to accomplish the feat once again and had already obtained my official shirt and shorts for the event. It never took place.

A few days before, on November 27, 1992, there had been a second attempt to overthrow the government. My most vivid memory was seeing a spokesman for the government on television telling the people to remain calm, that everything was under control. But listening to the radio at the same moment, we heard announcers screaming that the federal police were breaking down the doors of their studio and then the radio went silent. Shortly after, we saw military airplanes flying past our hillside and then explosions in the distance as they bombed the airport in the center of the city, the place from which the president would escape if he were to try to do so.

No, everything wasn't under control. And, although this coup was also short-lived, it left many more deaths than that of February 4. PROVEA has a partial list of 32 people who died, twelve of whom were simply executed by the government police or military.

There was also a massacre of at least 33 men that day in a major Caracas prison. The gates were opened and the prisoners, thinking they were free, ran out—only to be killed once they were outside.

In January 1993 I left Venezuela to go to El Salvador. There was more peace in El Salvador at that moment than there was in Venezuela. In Nueva Tacagua a catechist had been beaten one night and jailed by the police. Other catechists had been arrested for taking pictures of mothers and preschool children protesting because the school had not functioned for two years.

On another occasion the police, with their automatic weapons pointed at us, raided my pressed-cardboard shack one morning while I was meeting with other clergy in the area. Then one morning I awoke and noticed a hole in the tin roof. What remained of the bullet was on the floor, a few inches from my bed.

Before going to Nueva Tacagua I was told that, if I had to choose between joy and poverty, I should choose joy. The people had enough poverty all around them. I was beginning to lose my sense of humor, and for this reason, more than any other, I decided it was time to leave Nueva Tacagua. I spent four months in El Salvador and Guatemala and then returned for a few weeks to Venezuela. In June I left for the United States.

One day in September, I received a call from a neighbor in Nueva Tacagua. The ground beneath our neighborhood was beginning to crack. A few days later he called again. My shack and my neighbors' homes were gone, forever.

A Beautiful Miss Universe and a Dirty Election

I returned to Venezuela in August 1994. I was no longer a missionary or an active Catholic priest. I had married a Venezuelan woman at the end of July and had come back to begin a new life as an ordinary U.S. citizen living in a foreign country.

In the few months I was gone, much had happened in Venezuela. Carlos Andrés Pérez had been ousted from power in May 1993 and an interim president, Ramón Velásquez, was elected by the congress to serve until the impeachment process against Pérez had been completed.

In the December elections of that year, Rafael Caldera was re-elected president with about 30 percent of the votes. He had been president before, from 1969 to 1974. He had founded the COPEI (Comité de Organización Política Electoral Independiente, Christian Democrats) party but now he split from them when they did not choose him as their candidate. His new alliance with other parties was called *Convergencia,* but one could say that a *COPEIano* was back in power.

He had only been in office a few months when about half of the nation's banking system collapsed and its executives fled to Miami and other parts of the world. That left ordinary investors up in the air and the government with the responsibility of finding funds to repay what they had deposited.

As the 1998 elections were approaching, the two principal political parties were having problems deciding who their candidates would be. Since the overthrow of the dictator Marcos Pérez Jiménez in 1958, the AD (Acción Democrática, Social Democrats) and COPEI parties had dominated the political scene. It was commonly accepted that one or the other of these parties would always win the presidential elections, although many other parties existed in the country.

However, as the campaigning began, the leader in the polls was a former Miss Universe (1981), Irene Sáez. She had formed her own party, which simply bore her first name, IRENE. Caracas is divided into five municipalities, and she was the current mayor of the smallest one, a relatively wealthy area. Her beauty was indisputable; children thought she looked like the Barbie dolls that filled the toy stores. A local company even started producing "Irene" dolls.

The COPEI party, unable to come up with their own candidate and figuring that they would be betting on a sure winner, decided to give their backing to Ms. Sáez. She accepted the endorsement. It was like the kiss of death. Her popularity rapidly began to drop.

At the same time, Hugo Chávez began to appear on the political scene. He had been released from prison by President Caldera in 1994 and had traveled the country visiting with people. As his name began to rise in the polls, the ADecos and COPEIanos began to worry.

Another candidate also began to rise, Henrique Salas Römer. He had been governor of the state of Carabobo, a position that his son occupied after him. He, like Irene Sáez, had also formed his own party, Proyecto Venezuela.

As the election drew near, the only hope the traditional parties saw for their future was to unite against Chávez, and so they dropped their own candidates and threw their support to back Salas Römer.

This meant that the COPEI party abandoned Irene Sáez. Since these events took place days before the elections, it was impossible to change the ballots. But the Venezuelan presidential ballots contained photos of the candidates alongside the party identification. This meant that if you cast your ballot in the COPEI slot, which bore the photo of a former Miss Universe, your vote went for a middle-aged male, Henrique Salas Römer!

The campaigns were dirty, especially against Chávez. It was said that if Chávez won, there would be immediate devaluation of the Venezuelan currency.[12] Television ads tried to confuse people by linking Chávez to the massacre of February-March 1989 for which the ADeco president, Carlos Andrés Pérez, was responsible. The press forecast censorship if Chávez were elected and spread the word around the world.

Chávez's opposition was also well financed. One way the parties had stayed in power was with government funds. Depending on the number of votes they had received in the previous election, they were given government money to support their parties. Chávez's party, the MVR,[13] had no such aid.

The elections were held on December 6, 1998, and when the results started to indicate that Chávez had clearly won, there was rejoicing in the streets. The sky was full of fireworks. The air was full of music. The impossible had happened.

If someone were to ask me if I had ever seen a miracle in my lifetime, I would surely respond that it was the election of Hugo Chávez as president of Venezuela. To put the matter in U.S. terms, you would have to imagine the Republicans getting about one percent of the votes in a presidential election, the Democrats about two percent and a dark horse winning with almost sixty percent. It is an impossible concept outside of a dream world.

Chávez had campaigned on the need for a new constitution and for getting rid of corruption. The incredible break from the traditional parties was exhilarating. Newspapers would later say that the whole country was excited about the prospect of a new political environment. That, however, was not true. The music heard that night were songs of Alí Primera, a Venezuelan protest singer who died in a suspicious automobile accident in 1985. They were songs that had seldom been played on the radio but that were commonly heard in the barrios. The songs spoke of the oppression of the laborer, the struggles of the people in the developing world, the domination of the gringo over Latin America.

Chávez did have almost sixty percent of the vote. But forty percent of those who went to the polls that day did not vote for him and the music wasn't their favorite. There was hatred and anger in the minds of many Venezuelans on that December 6. These emotions were not noticed that night because of the sounds of celebration, but before long they would begin to surface. Forty years of concentrated power and corruption do not end with a single election.

Changing the Direction of the Ship

When Venezuelans awoke on the morning of December 7, 1998, many must have thought that the ship of state had taken a 180-degree turn the day before. But turning a ship with more than twenty million passengers and crew members on board was not going to be an easy task. And when that ship, fueled by corruption, had been going full speed for forty years, the work ahead was more a dream than a promised reality. Officers and crew were soon to change, but some people's mutinous desires would rapidly surface.

Chávez tried to show his plans symbolically by ordering a new presidential sash. The press criticized this as a strange expenditure of money by someone who was supposed to be a people's president. But Chávez did not want to wear the sash that had been handed down from one president to another, individuals whom he considered to be examples of years of corruption.

He also knew that the changes the country needed would not be possible without a new constitution. The current one had been enacted in 1961 and favored the traditional political parties.

Chávez had campaigned on the promise of a new constitution. To accomplish this, it would be necessary to call for a constitutional assembly, elect its members, and gain the approval of the result. None of this was assured when he took the oath of office on February 2, 1999. However, he was so sure that it would happen that when the moment for his inauguration arrived, he took the oath of office on "this dying constitution."

The referendum to hold a constitutional convention easily won approval. When the election of the members took place, those belonging to the "Patriotic Pole" that supported Chávez won overwhelmingly, gaining more than 90 percent of the seats. As the day for the referendum approached, the walls of the city were covered with "Sí's" and "No's". Finally,

48

on December 15 of that year, the voting to approve or reject the proposed constitution took place. But there was a problem that day.

It had been raining for weeks before the election and on December 15 the rain continued, making it difficult for some people to arrive at the polls before they closed. Since some had opened late because of the rain, it was decided to allow them to stay open for a few more hours. This seemed to be a reasonable decision on the part of the government. But a natural catastrophe was occurring, an event that happens only once in hundreds of years. The sides of the mountains between Caracas and the ocean began to break loose. As trees and boulders came tumbling down the almost mile-high mountainsides, they gained incredible force. High-rise buildings were cut in half; smaller dwellings were totally eliminated. People climbed onto roofs, running from one side to the other and finally dying in the tidal wave of mud sweeping everything in its path downward, into the ocean on one side and into Caracas on the other.

On December 16 and the days that followed, few people in Venezuela thought about the new constitution which had been approved by about 70 percent of those voting. As one looked at the television and saw an arm sticking out of the mud behind a news reporter, a street where the debris covered the telephone booths, or an aerial view of a neighborhood where friends or family had lived, the constitution was of little importance. Parents stood in lines to appear on television with photos of their children, asking if anyone had seen them; children appeared with photos of their parents, brothers, and sisters.

At one moment the International Red Cross estimated that maybe fifty thousand people died that night. Some weeks later, during an international flight between the United States and Venezuela, the news program on the airline mentioned one hundred thousand. Both figures may be exaggerated, but there can be no disputing that a multitude of people disappeared. They belonged to all socio-economic classes. Over forty thousand were airlifted out of the area in helicopters. Additional thousands walked into the ocean holding on to ropes in order to board military launches meant for landing troops on beachheads.

Traveling along the coast three years later, one could still see structures totally filled with mud. The sides of the mountains still looked as though a giant bear had walked through them, scratching out huge crevices with its claws.

The opposition criticized the government for what had happened because the polls were allowed to be open later that day. Only a year had passed since the presidential elections in 1998, but now the government was responsible for everything, even a tragedy of nature.

Soon the country would have to begin rebuilding: physically, to repair the damage of the landslides; psychologically, to deal with the loss of loved ones; and, politically, to begin implementing the new constitution. Life would go on.

Part of that life was a little blue book that people carried with them and would hold high in the air as they demonstrated in favor of the government: the new constitution.

I remember a woman on the street telling me, as a foreign reporter, how proud she was of the constitution. According to her, Venezuela was the only country in the world that had a constitution that had been approved by a vote of all the people. She felt it was her constitution.

But James Anderson, bureau chief for the Associated Press in Venezuela three years later, would not grant her that ownership. In an AP news release with his byline, he spoke of Chávez's "hand-crafted Venezuelan constitution." Did he forget that there was an election to have a constitutional convention? That, afterwards, there were elections to decide who would go to it? That finally there was an election to decide if the new constitution would be accepted? And that it was approved by about 70 percent of those voting in that election?

Seventy percent seems like an impressive percentage. But the opposition newspaper *El Universal,* (whose building also houses the Associated Press), would not see it that way. In a front-page editorial[14] three years later, they announced to the world that the constitution had been approved by only 21 percent of the electorate. Their reasoning went as follows: Only 30 percent of those eligible to vote had voted. 70 percent of 30 percent is 21 percent. In other words, a whopping 79 percent of the electorate had not voted for it.

On the one hand they were right. But by using the same reasoning we could also conclude that only 9 percent of the population was against the constitution (30 percent of the 30 percent who had voted). Actually, the 21 percent favorable vote was not far from the 24.6 percentage of the popular vote that George W. Bush received in 2000.

Another part of the reality was the fact that four major elections had been held in the course of thirteen months. Whether one was for or against the constitution, by the time the vote was held, many felt there was only one possible outcome: it would be approved. They were right. Chávez and his supporters were gaining strength.

In 2000, presidential elections would be held again under the new constitution. Only one viable candidate appeared, Francisco Arias Cárdenas. He had collaborated with Chávez in the 1992 attempted coup and spent time with him in prison. Even in prison they had had their differences. Now they were the principal opposing candidates for the presidency. Chávez won by an even higher percentage than he had in 1998.

2002, the Year with only 363 Days

In spite of the decisive victories in the elections, friction was mounting between Chávez and his opponents. Chávez was often caustic in his remarks about the elite and wealthy, and unrelenting in his criticism of the political opponents he had defeated. While his remarks might have been seen as valid by many of his supporters, others took them as insults. His words were also portrayed as beneath the dignity of a president. To say the least, they would definitely have to be considered politically unwise.

By October 2001, Donna Hrinak, the U.S. ambassador to Venezuela, admitted to the press that Venezuelan politicians had contacted her seeking help from the U.S. to oust Chávez. Then in November Chávez issued a series of forty-nine laws that provoked the opposition. The charge was that there had not been enough consultation before enacting them, but the reality was that they affected the previous rights of business people, large fishing companies, and big landholders. A few weeks later, in December, there was a one-day work stoppage, strangely backed by the leadership of both the big business federation and the biggest labor organization. It would be the prelude for many such actions in the months to follow.

The year 2002 began with massive demonstrations against the government and equally huge ones in favor of it. Most of the opposition's efforts were well publicized in advance. But some gave the appearance of being "spontaneous," like when a colonel on active duty called for the resignation of the president and suddenly found himself a hero. Making his proclamation from a five-star hotel, he was then whisked to a plaza in the wealthy part of the city while television screens invited the public to come and show their support for him.

From the plaza the multitude marched to the home of the president, the Casona. Only the president's wife and children were in the house at the time, but they lived through some terrifying moments as upper-class people tried to attack the home, destroying a nearby playground as their fury developed.

On April 6, Carlos Ortega of the CTV (the largest labor union) announced a "strike" for Tuesday, April 9. It again had the support of FEDECAMARAS (which represents big business), but this time it was also backed by the leadership of PDVSA (Petróleos de Venezuela, Sociedad Anónima), the national petroleum company of Venezuela.

The strangeness of this "strike" should be noted. PDVSA workers were known to be among the best paid in the country. Why would the best-paid workers in the country want to strike? Better salaries? Better working conditions? No. They were unhappy because Chávez had appointed a new president and board of directors for PDVSA who were not to their liking.

Their cry was for a continuation of the "meritocracy." They didn't want the government meddling in who would control PDVSA. Their position was that the people who should run PDVSA were those who had worked there, who understood the oil industry, and who had earned their positions within the company. PDVSA, they said, was known for the quality and efficiency of its employees.

But while the employees of PDVSA saw themselves in this light and projected this image of "independence" and "merit" through the friendly commercial media, others saw the image of a "black box" which hid many secrets inside. Later, I will treat this question in greater detail.

The strike that began April 9, continued another day, then another. On April 11 a march of solidarity with the strikers was scheduled. It was to go from the Plaza Altamira, which had become the central meeting point for the opposition, to the headquarters of PDVSA in another part of the city, Chuao. But the march took a turn, a fatal turn. The leaders of the demonstration began encouraging the people to march on the presidential palace, Miraflores.[15]

No approval had been given for such a route, and the planners would have known that no such approval would be given. Supporters of the government had occupied that part of the city regularly. Any march in that direction would surely lead to confrontation.

As the private television stations gave continuous coverage of the event, more and more people allied with the opposition poured out of their homes and onto the super-highway leading into the center of the city. At the same time, government supporters, seeing what was happening, began to fill the areas near the presidential palace.

Puente Llaguno, a bridge that is a few blocks from Miraflores and overlooks a principal downtown street leading to the palace (Avenida Baralt), was full of government supporters as the marchers began to approach. Suddenly shots rang out. Snipers from the surrounding buildings were firing into the crowd of supporters. As the crowd ran from the bridge, police from the street below who were providing protection for the opposition marchers also opened fire. Quickly the bridge emptied as the occupants scurried to the two sides, hoping for protection from the surrounding buildings.

Then television cameras captured a scene that would be repeated thousands of times in the coming months. Three men with handguns began to return fire from the bridge. One was a city councilman.

Reviewing the scenes of the event, one would logically conclude that the men were responding to the threat posed by the shooting from the snipers and the police. The range of their handguns would seem to have been incapable of reaching the opposition marchers who were still a few blocks distant.

But the opposition would speak of the "Massacre of Miraflores" (in U.S. terms, "The White House Massacre") and would show the video of these three government supporters shooting. Almost never would they or the commercial media show photos of the police firing into the crowd. These photos appeared only in alternative publications.

However, even before this confrontation happened, a strange thing was occurring in another part of the city. In front of a CNN reporter, a group of high-ranking military officials were announcing that there were dead bodies in the streets and these officials called for the president to step down. This, before a single shot had been fired!

By early morning, April 12, they must have felt that their objectives had been accomplished. General Lucas Rincón had been pressured into announcing that the president had been asked to resign and had accepted. Then President Chávez was arrested and removed from the presidential palace. At 4:51 a.m., Pedro Carmona Estanga, president of FEDECAMARAS, announced that he would assume the presidency of the country as part of a transitional civil-military government.

The coup leaders had taken the government television and radio stations off the air earlier and so the only information available to the public was being broadcast by the commercial stations. Their euphoria was boundless. These stations and their owners had been hoping for such an event for months, and their announcers were even proud to tell how they had helped in the preparations for the coup and had been congratulated by leaders for their work.

In the course of the day, they had a wealth of precious scenes to share. Well-dressed people attacked the Cuban embassy, thinking that maybe President Chávez was inside. They cut off the electricity and water. They destroyed automobiles outside. As was mentioned before, Caracas is divided into five districts, each with its own local mayor. Two mayors were supporters of Chávez; three were not. One of the opposition mayors, Henrique Capriles Radonsky, wanted to search the embassy, to which the ambassador responded that Cuba had resisted the invasion of the United States for forty years, so how did they expect him to permit an invasion by one person?

Government officials were arrested and beaten by onlookers as the police were taking them away.

At 5:30 p.m. in the presidential palace, Carmona Estanga proclaimed himself president in front of an elegant crowd of the Venezuelan elite.. They greeted the initial decrees of the new government with smiles and enthusiastic applause. The Congress (dominated by Chávez supporters) was disbanded. So was the Supreme Tribunal of Justice.[16] The attorney general, the public defender, the mayors and governors of the country were also removed from office. The name of the republic was changed to what it had been before the new constitution. The constitution, which had been approved by 70 percent of the voters only a few years before, was gone.

But a few hours earlier, the attorney general had announced that Chávez had not resigned. That morning, a storybook event had taken place. Shortly after his arrest, two young women lieutenants managed to speak to the president. The colonel in charge was still sleeping, and they knew the soldier guarding the president who let them through. Chávez's first words to one of them were, "Look, my child, I want to tell you something: I am still president and I have not resigned." At that moment the colonel caught the women. He was shirtless and angry. Who had let them in? Frightened by their experience, they nevertheless communicated with someone who was in touch with the attorney general.

Gradually members of the military, who had been following orders from superiors, began to realize what was happening.

During the night, Chávez had been moved to another military base where a young corporal managed to make contact with him. In an article that appeared in *Ultimas Noticias* a year later, the corporal said, "I asked him if he had resigned." Chávez replied that he had never resigned and never would. The corporal told him to get some paper, write down what he had just said, and put it in the trash basket. He then returned, collected the trash, and managed to get the note to higher officers.

The ordinary citizen was also reacting. I spoke to one woman who said she cried the whole night, wondering what was happening to "my president." On Saturday morning, April 13, thousands of ordinary people started surrounding military installations and were marching in the direction of Miraflores. With most of them armed only with their bodies, they had poured out of the hillsides and walked miles to protest what had taken place.

Then the high command of the air base in Maracay signed a document for the "Rescue of the National Dignity." Other officers joined in.

Around 1:30 p.m., the new cabinet officers were supposed to be sworn in, but a notice that they should abandon the area interrupted the ceremony. Video footage shows them hurrying out of the palace, their faces bewildered at what was happening.

In the late afternoon, Carmona announced changes to the decrees he had announced the day before. They had gone too far, but it was now too late. Shortly after 10 p.m., he announced his resignation and recognized the vice-president of the Chávez government as president.

Chávez had been moved to a Venezuelan island, La Orchila. Helicopters had been sent to bring him back to Caracas. In the middle of the night, at 2:50 a.m. on Sunday, April 14, 2002, a helicopter returned Chávez to the presidential palace as thousands in the streets below cried and cheered.

The commercial radio and TV stations had already stopped broadcasting any news of what had happened the day before. So as to keep the ordinary citizen in the dark, they showed only cartoons and old movies. That night, the major dailies did not go to press, becoming accomplices in the news blackout as well.

But the media conspiracy was only beginning. For the next year it was as though the installation of the dictator Carmona had never happened. The only scenes of those forty-eight hours from April 11 to April 13 shown repeatedly were of the three men firing handguns from the bridge. They, and the democratically elected government that they supported, were the only ones to blame for the "Miraflores massacre." The almost forty-eight hours of dictatorship never happened. 2002, in Venezuela, was the year that had only 363 days.

Caracas, April 11-14, 2002

I was not in Venezuela while the coup was taking place, and my description of the events in the last chapter is based on research. But my wife, Susana, was in Caracas at the time, and when I returned she shared what she had seen and experienced. The following are her words:

"The days immediately before the coup were very tense. We all knew something was going to happen, but we didn't know what. Friends were maintaining a twenty-four hour watch around Miraflores. Some had even set up tents and were sleeping there.

"The opposition had organized a march on April 11 that was supposed to end at the offices of PDVSA in Chuao. On that day I went with a friend to sell art supplies but, as we drove along the divided highway through the center of Caracas, we saw that the opposition march had taken a detour from its original route. We had already heard about that on the radio, but when we actually saw it, we decided to go to Puente Llaguno. Quite frankly, I was tired of all the marches and had planned not to go. But seeing the violent attitude of the opposition and the fact that they were marching toward the presidential palace, we also changed our plans. We knew there were going to be problems.

"We left the car with another friend and went to Miraflores. There we encountered a multitude of people. I think it was about midday when the confrontation began between the Metropolitan Police[17] and those who were supporting the government.

"The National Guard was there to protect Miraflores from the opposition demonstrators who were advancing toward it and toward us—at least that's what we thought. The marchers were still five or six blocks away, but the Metropolitan Police were moving ahead of the march and were trying to open a way through the National Guard so that the demonstrators could reach the presidential palace.

"We who were supporting the government had absolutely nothing with which to defend ourselves from the police. Eventually we broke chunks of cement off a wall to have something to throw at them.

"Then shots rang out. We were under the bridge on Avenida Baralt, running toward the Metropolitan Police and then away from them. Back and forth, forth and back, but with nothing much to defend ourselves with. At that moment we began to sense the presence of snipers, and we could see that the shots were coming from the fourth or fifth floor of the Hotel Eden. I wish I could tell you exactly where but with all the violence I saw that afternoon and evening, it is difficult to describe precisely many details, such as the exact hour when things happened. I don't even remember when it was daylight and when it became night.

"When we went up on the bridge, I saw a man being shot in the head by one of the snipers, Others carried him away, leaving a pool of blood behind. They ran to a temporary first-aid stand that had been set up by Miraflores. Everyone else on the bridge fell to the ground.

"Finally getting off the bridge, we went back to Avenida Baralt below, and I saw about six people who had been wounded. But the Metropolitan Police kept shooting and were not permitting others to remove the wounded from the street. The men would run back and forth, trying to help them, ducking behind the newsstands for protection. It was for this reason that three government supporters who did have handguns in their possession started shooting in the direction of the police to distract them.

"I remember seeing one youth who had been shot in the head. Nobody could reach him. There he was, sprawled in the street, and I have no idea whether he lived or died.

"We spent hours there. One time when I was lying on the ground I started using my cellular phone to communicate with close friends and relatives. I really thought I was going to die that day. My own father simply responded, "You

&@#% assassin," and hung up the phone. He had been listening to the story that the television commentators were telling, which was totally contrary to what I was experiencing.

"At another moment we heard President Chávez through the loudspeakers in the area. He was delivering a nationwide broadcast, telling people to be calm, that nothing was happening. I felt deceived at that moment, as though we were just cannon fodder. I know that it was important to urge people to be calm, but his remarks didn't have anything to do with what we were experiencing at that moment either.

"Throughout the afternoon, people were saying that armaments were coming so that we could help defend Miraflores, but that never happened. I saw Javier from La Vega.[18] He seemed so depressed, totally contrary to his usual attitude. I told him what I had heard about the weapons that were supposedly coming. He replied, 'I will not take up arms. If they want to kill me, they can. But I am not going to kill anybody.' He was crying, super-depressed, totally defeated. He had come with a group of mostly old people from La Vega. By accident they came upon a march for the opposition where a woman in that crowd threw acid in the face of one of the elderly men that Javier was accompanying, burning his face completely. Javier, a dedicated activist, was despondent.

"I do not remember how many wounded I saw that afternoon, but there were a lot. Every few minutes I saw someone being carried away by *compañeros*.

"I remember one moment when I was about two blocks away from the bridge and I was saying to the National Guard, 'Protect us! Protect us!' They were there just like statues, doing absolutely nothing. They didn't defend us nor did they do anything to stop the massacre that was going on. They were just like statues!

"I think six or seven hours passed like this. One time when we went back on the bridge I said to my friend, 'Let's go eat something. I'm hungry.' I hadn't eaten since that morning. We went to a nearby restaurant and there was a television set. When we began to eat, the head of the National Guard, Alberto Camacho Kairuz, made an announcement in support of the opposition. I said to my friend, 'We're sunk.' Without finishing our food, we left to see what was happening. That's when we saw the National Guard retreating.

"We then understood the seriousness of the situation. Nobody could explain to us what was happening. We didn't know at that moment about the coup that was underway. Then I got hit in the back of my neck with *perdigones*.[19] Luckily, I was some distance away and they just left scars on my neck. At least they were not imbedded in the skin. And, even more fortunately, they were not bullets. I would be dead today.

"During the afternoon, the supporters of the government began painting red stripes on their faces with lipstick to distinguish themselves from the opposition, although the opposition was really never that close. When I saw tapes of the television reporting afterwards, it looked as if the conflict had been with the opposition marchers. The struggle had really been with the Metropolitan Police.

"I know now that on the other side of Miraflores there was another battlefield, and the opposition did get closer to the Presidential Palace. That, too, was done with the help of the Metropolitan Police. That still irks me: that the police would march at the head of a demonstration against the government. We saw very clearly how they took out their revolvers and shot at the people.

"The National Guard was supposedly there to protect the Presidential Palace from the opposition. They had made a kind of human chain across the street. But when they left, that opened the way for the police to go through.

"We left that street, too, and I was sitting on the divider in the middle of Avenida Urdaneta which passes over the bridge. At that moment I said to my friend, 'One feels like cannon fodder. How can we defend ourselves? Something strange is going on.' We still didn't know what.

"While we were talking, I saw a couple of men talking to each other about thirty feet from me. We thought the worst had passed, since we didn't hear any more shooting. But then one of the men fell to the ground. I said to my friend, 'Look at that! Those people don't even know what has gone on today. How is it possible that anyone could get drunk in this kind of situation?' I hadn't finished what I was saying when the other man fell to the ground also. Someone had shot them, but no shots were heard. They had evidently used silencers.

"That's when we decided we had to get out of there. It was about eight o'clock at night. We wanted to go one way, but because of the presence of the Metropolitan Police and the opposition, we went another way. Fortunately someone came along in a car, recognized us, and gave us a ride to where we had parked our car.

"There we met a person who had participated in the march of the opposition and was truly upset because she felt she had been manipulated that day.

"We got home at about midnight, dazed from all that had happened that day. It seemed unbelievable.

"The next morning, Friday, April 12, we spent a lot of time in a cyber-café trying to send information to other parts of the world about what was happening. I cried several times. I think I spent a good part of the day crying.

"We also tried to help other friends whose lives were in danger because of their political involvement, not exactly to hide them but to be sure they were in safe areas. They were doing all they could to communicate with others they knew in the government, letting them know that they were not renouncing their allegiance to the government and urging them to do the same. We knew their lives were in danger from what we had seen on television.

"It was not only horrible to watch the television stations rejoicing in the antigovernment position that they had promoted for so long, but the images they presented as well. All day long they were looking for government officials and even beating them when they were arrested. All this was being televised. They took the camera crews with them to show this!

"It was like a Roman circus where the Christians were thrown to the lions, or a modern witch-hunt. It was all being electronically transmitted for the delight of the opposition.

"It is hard remembering all that happened those days, but I know that Friday I cried and cried and cried.

"The next day, April 13, we felt we had to do something more. About midday I left home with my friend, knowing absolutely nothing about what was happening due to the self-imposed media blackout. They were showing only cartoons and old movies. The only radio station that had any information was Radio Fé y Alegría and we listened to old people crying all day long, wanting to know what was happening to their president.

"But as we were going down the road, we saw a multitude of people emerging from the barrios. They had portable megaphones and were urging everyone to march to the presidential palace. They kept repeating: "Todos a Miraflores! Everyone to Miraflores!" The size of the crowd that was developing was incredible. It was like a human river going down the mountainside.

"Another means of communication was cellular phones. All day we received messages. 'Go to Miraflores!' 'Go to Fuerte Tiuna!'[20] 'Chávez hasn't resigned!'

"We crowded as many people as possible into the car, and we drove as far as we could toward Miraflores. The people were euphoric. It was like a huge celebration. When we arrived, the soldiers on the roof of the Casa Militar[21] (which overlooks the presidential palace) were taking off their black berets, throwing them away, and replacing them with red ones.[22] They were waving a huge Venezuelan flag and holding their rifles in the air triumphantly. The hair on my arms stood up.

"Some friends had been there since the evening before. I have a friend who lives near the palace—he said that since the beginning of the coup he heard people shouting, '¡Viva Chávez!' '¡Viva Chávez!' But the media had said nothing about this. Until we arrived, we had no idea about the mass of people who were there.

"It was an unreal celebration. The people were singing and dancing. They were joking with the soldiers. Then I saw Javier from La Vega. He was a totally different person from the Javier I had seen two days before. We hugged and jumped with joy.

"And the number of people! They kept coming and coming and coming. If you looked down Avenida Urdaneta there was no end to the number of people who were there.[23]

"When the helicopter carrying Chávez arrived in the middle of the night, I had goose bumps on my skin. Though I had supported the political changes of the previous four years, I was not personally infatuated with Chávez, so it was not his presence that caused this response. But the reaction of the people, the sense that they were the ones who had made the moment happen, made it an experience that I will never forget. People were fainting, were delirious, were crying with emotion. The happiness they were experiencing after being totally defeated the day before was indescribable. It was a tremendous day, truly a tremendous day."

Frankfurt, Germany, April 12, 2002

While Susana was in downtown Caracas watching people being shot and receiving *perdigones* in her neck from the Metropolitan Police, I was in the air between Denver, Colorado, Washington, D.C., and Frankfurt, Germany, watching movies and being served meals by flight attendants.

At the beginning of April, I had left Venezuela to visit Austria. I had not seen my ninety-three-year-old aunt in twenty-five years and had planned the trip long before. That is not to say that Susana and I were not worried about what was going to happen in Venezuela. There was so much tension and so much maneuvering on the part of the opposition that the probability of a coup seemed high. We had also talked about what we should do if one did happen. Leaving the country was among the possibilities.

Were we greatly involved in the political process of Venezuela? No. Susana had recently joined a neighborhood Bolivarian Circle, and neighbors knew we were in favor of the current government, but that was the extent of any involvement. However, we both knew enough about the history of right-wing coups in Latin America to be worried. The forty-eight hours of the Carmona government proved that our concern was justified.

I stopped in the United States for a few days and then, on April 11, I set out on my journey to Austria. Landing in Frankfurt the morning of April 12, I took the subway from the airport to the train station in the center of the city, checked into a hotel, and then returned to the street. It was then that I saw the newspapers announcing that President Chávez had resigned.

I ran to telephone Susana. It was impossible to get through. I thought about trying to make a reservation and returning to Venezuela as quickly as possible.

I had submitted a no-longer-current article to a U.S. newspaper about the situation in Venezuela, and so I called the editor. He asked me, "Is your family ok?" With that I broke down crying. I was thinking of Susana. I was remembering friends. Were they alive? Were they safe? I stood in the middle of the sidewalk at a public telephone, speechless, tears rolling down my face. I muttered, "Please don't hang up. I'm still here. I just need a moment."

The man apologized for having asked the question. I thanked him for having asked. Maybe it was good that I didn't know where Susana was. If I had known, I might not have been able to continue the conversation.

Watching the international news on television later that day, I heard that Chávez's daughter had announced in Cuba that he had not resigned. I decided to go on to Vienna, visit my aunt in a small village nearby, and then return to Venezuela immediately.

On Sunday morning, April 14, I arrived in my mother's birthplace in time for breakfast. Rabensberg, Austria, is a small town with one main street; people leave their bicycles at the train station when they go to Vienna to work. While I was sitting at the kitchen table with my cousins, my aunt came from her room. "You live in Venezuela," she said. "I see on television that Chávez is back in power."

It was hard to believe. I decided to stay the night in Rabensburg, and I spent the day with my cousins, telling the story of Venezuela—and crying. I had so many pent-up emotions. In many ways I was probably vicariously experiencing the joy of the people in front of Miraflores when Chávez's helicopter soared overhead. After feeling total defeat the day before, it seemed to me that the whole situation had changed.

When I finally got in touch with Susana, she told me that there was no need to hurry back to Venezuela. At that moment maybe I could do more for the country within the United States..

I stayed two days in Vienna, instead of ten, and returned to Cheyenne. There I saw an editorial—"Venezuela's Chávez must be confronted"—in the *Wyoming Tribune-Eagle* by Myriam Marquez of the *Orlando Sentinel*. In her editorial, she tried to portray Chávez as a dictator.

I contacted the newspaper and they published an op-ed I wrote rebutting Ms. Marquez's piece. An east-coast journalist friend recommended that I also send it to the *Orlando Sentinel,* but when I contacted them I was given the impression that anyone who would write something in favor of the Chávez government was off his rocker.

At the same time, an online newspaper, Vheadline.com, contacted me to ask if they could reprint my editorial. I don't know how they had gotten hold of it, but with that my life took a turn.

For forty years I had tried to be an advocate for the oppressed throughout the world. But after marrying I'd had little time for anything except trying to make a bit of money so we could survive. Susana and I had done this by starting a small business selling art supplies. It had kept us alive.

I had written little and published nothing for nine years, but in light of all the negative reporting in the U.S. press I decided that I should try to put my writing talents to work in favor of the peaceful revolution that was happening in Venezuela. I decided to drop out of the art supply business, put aside enough money to pay the credit card bills for ten months, and start writing full time. With my social security check and a few days of contract work for a foreign company in Venezuela each month, I figured I could survive and gradually pay off the credit card debt.

I turned on the computer, touched the keys, and became a writer once again.

The Search for Peace, My Piece

Upon being restored to power, Chávez changed. His rhetoric was less provocative. He no longer wore a military uniform. He reappointed the old board members of PDVSA, whose replacement had been the immediate cause of the strike leading up to the coup. He acknowledged that he had made mistakes, and he called for dialog.

The mechanism he proposed for these conversations was "dialog tables" which would take place among all sectors and in all parts of the country.

The opposition, on the other hand, showed little interest in dialog. Their attitude following the coup seemed to follow the maxim I had learned as a little child: If at first you don't succeed, try, try again.

The dialog tables began their meetings. But FEDECAMARAS, the CTV, and the representatives of the commercial mass media all dropped out. There could be no dialog with only one part of the proposed conversation present.

The opposition united to form a group called the Coordinadora Democrática (the Democratic Coordination). It was never clear to the public who belonged to it, who could belong, or how the leadership had been chosen. For a while, Antonio Ledezma, a former governor of Caracas who had lost in the last municipal election to a Chávez supporter, seemed to be the spokesperson. But by December Carlos Ortega of the CTV, Carlos Fernández of FEDECAMARAS, and Juan Fernández (an active executive of the national petroleum company, PDVSA) were the principal spokespersons. It should be noted that none of these represented a political party, although parties participated in the Coordinadora.

The opposition wanted facilitators from outside of Venezuela. The government invited Jimmy Carter. He came after the Carter Center in Atlanta, Georgia, had accepted the invitation. But the fact that it was the government that had issued the invitation made his presence unacceptable. The opposition had wanted the Organization of American States.

Part of the problem the government had with the OAS was the reaction of their Interamerican Commission for Human Rights to the April coup. During the short time Carmona was in power, the Commission had communicated with him, thereby giving recognition to his government. It urged respect for human rights but nowhere spoke of the problem of overthrowing a legitimately elected government. It also made no plea for protection of President Chávez, who had been kidnapped.

Nevertheless, the government finally invited the OAS and the United Nations to join the Carter Center in the facilitation process. Their first joint statement spoke of the need to find a solution in keeping with the constitution. The opposition was not happy. Carlos Fernández, President of FEDECAMARAS, said in the daily *El Nacional* that the opposition was only interested in meeting with international organizations to discuss how Chávez would leave the presidency.

Eventually César Gaviria, former president of Colombia and secretary general of the OAS at the time, came to Venezuela to assume leadership of the dialogs.

While this was going on, 2002 was marked by demonstrations and counter demonstrations. The opposition commemorated the 11th of every month, supporters of the government every 13th. In between, other reasons were found to be in the streets, trying to show who could gather more people. As the year went on, enthusiasm waned on both sides.

Then, in October, some active generals who had been favorable to the coup called for the resignation of the president. They set up a camp in Plaza Altamira and, encouraged by their admirers, roughed it in the five-star hotels that border the Plaza. They appeared regularly to give pep talks and to issue a call to other officers to follow them.

A few did. It should be kept in mind that the Venezuelan military had more than two hundred generals and admirals. Those involved did not command troops, and their action seemed to have little force within the military.

Another "strike" was called by the CTV for October 21. Carlos Ortega, the CTV president, said that afternoon the "strike" was 83.72 percent complete. It was a ridiculous number with that .72, but so was the word *paro* (strike) since it was really more of a lockout of the workers.

Then another "strike" was called for December 2, an open-ended strike. This one lasted for the two months surrounding the Christmas and New Year holidays. It was, again, a lockout by the upper-middle class and the wealthy, who shut down their businesses and their factories so that their employees could not work. It also principally affected the wealthy areas of the city where upper-class hooligans threatened shopkeepers who opened their establishments. In these parts of the city, people had to stand in line to enter supermarkets that opened for only a few hours each morning to supply the basic necessities of their inhabitants, including the wines and gourmet items which supermarkets in those parts of the city carry.

But in the popular areas of the city, commerce went on as usual after the first few days. The wealthy thought the "strike" was successful because they felt the effects where they lived and the commercial television stations gave ample coverage to those areas.

Every evening there was a news conference in front of the banner of one of Caracas's five-star hotels. Carlos Ortega of the CTV, Carlos Fernández of FEDECAMARAS, and Juan Fernández of PDVSA talked at length about how the "strike" was succeeding. They would announce antigovernment demonstrations for the coming days, and they filled the air with diatribes against the government.

As Christmas approached, a common greeting among opponents of the government was, "May you have a Merry

Christmas—without Chávez." On Christmas Eve, while the government channel covered a special Mass led by a Venezuelan bishop and the Pope's Mass from the Vatican, a commercial station broadcast a celebration of the opposition in Plaza Altamira. It showed people dancing to the tune of "Jingle Bells" while beating on pots and pans, the symbol of opposition to the government. The song has no relevance to the ordinary Venezuelan, but would be significant to those who had passed former Christmases in the United States. In many ways it was very appropriate.

Carlos Ortega had urged people not to celebrate Christmas on December 25 but to wait until January when Chávez would surely be gone. That had the unhappy sound of a statement a Grinch might make. So, on the 28th of December, the Coordinadora Democrática sponsored a party for the children of the city, seemingly unaware that the 28th is the day when Christians commemorate the killing of little children by Herod at the time of Christ's birth.

In many ways it didn't really matter because most people went on with their celebration of Christmas and the sky on New Year's Eve was more filled with fireworks than ever, partly because the opposition also put on a massive display that night.

For two months, the people lived without Coca-Cola and Pepsi-Cola while discovering once again the delicious homemade Venezuelan fruit drinks. They also lived without beer, drinking other alcoholic beverages. But one thing that did affect everyone was the strike by the petroleum executives and workers. This truly was a strike, but it had nothing to do with salaries or employee benefits. As I mentioned previously, the petroleum workers were among the best-paid employees in the nation.

At 4:00 p.m. on December 30, I placed my car at the end of a line waiting for gasoline at a nearby station. I went to sleep in the car at about 2:30 a.m. At 5 o'clock someone knocked on my window and soon after I was able to buy gasoline. That this could happen in the country that is one of the world's largest petroleum exporters shows the determination of the executives and employees of PDVSA, together with the elite of the country, to overthrow Chávez at any price. There was sabotage of oil installations and the computer software needed to operate them. Passwords were changed so that loyal employees could not use the equipment.

Private schools and many Catholic Church-sponsored schools had also joined in the "strike," and some public schools under the direction of opposition political leaders did, too. But many parents began to get tired of having their children at home, and some even took control of the schools and starting teaching the children themselves since the teachers didn't want to do so. A UNICEF spokesperson pointed out how even in situations of war, the education of children should continue. Her plea didn't faze the opposition.

But, gradually, the "strike" began to fizzle. Days passed, then weeks, then almost two months, and Chávez was still going strong. Everyone began to get tired. On February 2, 2003, there was a massive *firmazo* (signing) of petitions to remove Chávez. But the Coordinadora Democrática couldn't even agree on how they wanted to do it or what they wanted signed. The suggestions included outright refusal to recognize Chávez as president; a call for a constitutional amendment (changing the term of the president from six to four years); a recall referendum; another constitutional assembly (to get rid of the constitution approved by 70 percent of the voters just three years before); plus six other items. The idea was to have signatures for whatever they might decide to do in the future. They also said in their ads that such action was legal, constitutional, and binding, but the binding part had already been called into question.

I don't know if the strike was ever called off. It simply failed. Chávez would call it the second coup, an economic one. Within a few weeks, a judge ordered the arrest of Carlos Ortega, Carlos Fernández, and Juan Fernández. Only Carlos

Fernández was taken into custody and placed under house arrest. Then another judge freed them all on a technicality, to the great rejoicing of the opposition.

Once again, the only political prisoners were four government supporters. They were finally released in April after almost a year of imprisonment. With their release, the opposition said that this went to show there was no justice in Venezuela.

Jimmy Carter, George W. Bush:
We Hate Both of You

The coup had failed; the dissident military officials camped in Plaza Altamira seemed irrelevant; the two-month-long strike had fizzled. Chávez was still president. The constitution of 1999 had provided a new mechanism for citizen participation and control over elected officials: a referendum midway through the official's term. Even the president was included. Chávez often reminded the opposition of this option. It was a constitutional way to oust him.

Only 20 percent of the electorate had to petition for such a referendum, and Chávez's midterm was to be in August 2003. After months of negotiations, the opposition finally accepted the challenge. But instead of taking place in August 2003, the referendum finally happened a year later on August 15, 2004. And when it was over with, Chávez had won by about two million votes. Some members of the opposition immediately shouted "fraud" and refused to accept the results in spite of the presence of a multitude of international observers including Jimmy Carter and César Gaviria (Secretary General of the OAS) who recognized the results as valid. Anger ran so high that wealthy diners in a high-class Caracas restaurant beat on their plates in rejection of Jimmy Carter when he went to eat there. Ironically, even the government of the United States was blamed for the Chávez victory in spite of the fact that it had funneled millions of dollars into opposition groups to help them get rid of him!

The opposition was never in favor of the referendum. They could gather hundreds of thousands of people for their rallies in Caracas, and this seemed like impressive evidence that the majority of Venezuelans were against Chávez. However, as I traveled the country asking people their opinions, I could find little change from the voting patterns of 1998. I concluded that if a referendum were to be held, Chávez would win again by a 60-40 margin, which is what happened.

I also felt that the opposition leaders must have had the same information, although the surveys published in the commercial media often put Chávez's popularity at only about thirty percent or less.

The referendum didn't happen in August 2003 partly because it was the first time such a procedure had been planned and there was no set mechanism for collecting the necessary signatures. As I mentioned in the previous chapter, the opposition had gathered signatures in February 2003, months before a referendum was possible, but the National Electoral Council (CNE) questioned the validity of the process and the authenticity of the signatures. After the Council had decided the norms, signatures were gathered in November 2003. It took a few weeks for the opposition to turn them over to the CNE, which discovered cases where one person had filled in the personal information on many pages, followed supposedly by different signatures. Many signatures appeared to have been falsified. There was also the problem of signatures of dead people and of foreigners not eligible to vote.

The opposition said that they had almost four million signatures. But only 1,836,853 were recognized as valid by the CNE. 2,436,083 were needed for a presidential referendum. They were about 600,000 short. There was an outcry from the opposition.

To give the opposition the opportunity to validate the doubtful signatures, a "re-signing" was scheduled during which people whose signatures had been called into question could verify their authenticity. At the end of the process, the CNE announced that 2,451,821 signatures were acceptable (a mere 15,737 more than needed) and the referendum could take place. The August 15 date was set.

Many government supporters doubted the validity of the

decision. After the National Electoral Council announced that there were sufficient signatures for the presidential referendum, there were some outbursts of violence, supposedly by supporters of the government, to protest the alleged fraud in the collection of some of the signatures.

Was it government supporters who burned vehicles and fired shots at the offices of Alfredo Peña, the opposition mayor of greater Caracas? Possibly, but not inevitably. Was there foul play involved in the collection and counting of the signatures? Very possibly, but who knew?

The truth will probably never be known, but that evening President Chávez went on national television and accepted the decision of the Electoral Council. After standing in front of a painting of Jesus, he moved to those of the national heroes, Simon Bolívar and Antonio José de Sucre. Finally he ended his remarks next to a bust of Ezequiel Zamora. The setting provided a dramatic contrast to the frequent press conferences of the opposition. These usually took place with only the name of the classy five-star hotel as a backdrop.

It was with Zamora in mind that he projected himself into the future and announced the new "Battle of Santa Inés". In 1859 Zamora gave the federal army the impression that his troops were retreating. They succeeded in their strategy, turned around, and conquered their enemy.

Chávez was a master in front of the television camera. His presentation that night was a collage of key aspects of himself: friend, teacher, magician, politician, and strategist. At one moment viewers could imagine that they were in the middle of an intimate conversation with him. Then it was as though they were in a classroom learning about the history of the country.

He even pulled a surprise out of an old hat. The magic occurred when Chávez shared a five-year-old videotape with his audience. Everyone who didn't rely on the commercial mass media knew that Chávez was the person who had suggested the idea of putting the referendum into the constitution. The mass media, however, always presented him as being the main opponent of the referendum. But very few people could remember the speech Chávez had presented to the constitutional convention in 1999. This Chávez now showed in the video. At that time he had not only promoted the referendum but even suggested that only 10 percent of the voting population should be able to call for one, not the 20 percent that the constitution now requires.[24]

From the video viewing, his supporters were off to a political rally where he took a few moments to launch some barbs against his opponents. Finally, he announced his strategy, which came to be known as the Plan Maisanta, named after a Venezuelan hero. Each voting place was to have a UBE (Unidad de Batalla Electoral—an Electoral Battle Unit) that would organize *patrullas* (patrols). These would contact everyone in their areas to enlist their support for the government.

The night of August 14-15, I slept in the home of a coordinator of a UBE. Weeks of organization had gone into planning for this day. In her home she had a list of every voter in her zone and which persons the *patrullas* had contacted. I wanted to observe first hand the results of the Plan Maisanta.

At 3:00 a.m. I was awakened by the sound of fireworks, and I could hear a bugle in the distance. It was "the Diana," the term used here for reveille. By 3:30 a.m., the phone rang, and then my hostess began calling her patrol members.

At 3:50 a.m. we were in the car and rounding up workers to take their stations outside the polling place. Was the food ready for their breakfasts? she asked. Were the volunteers with vehicles ready to take people to vote?

When we arrived at the polling place at 4:26 a.m., twenty-nine people were already standing in line. The polls were scheduled to open at 7:00 a.m. I asked the first person in line if he would tell me for whom he was going to vote. Yes, "the comandante" (Chávez). Did he belong to any political party?

He said he had been a Communist all his life. Was Chávez a Communist? I asked. "No," he replied, "I wish he were."

(By chance, two days later I spoke to another man on the street who also said that he was a lifelong Communist Party member. His response to my question about Chávez and Communism was the same. Chávez had said on a number of occasions that he was not a Communist but a Bolivarian, although he had nothing against the Communists. His enemies liked to accuse him of being one.)

By 6:15 a.m. about 250 people were waiting to vote. The scene reminded me of the lines that form in the United States on the morning after Thanksgiving in front of the discount stores. I had never seen people so enthusiastic about the opportunity to vote.

I spent a few hours asking individuals and groups to share their opinions and to tell me how they were planning to vote. When I asked what would happen the next day if their side lost the referendum, all said they would accept the results. Throughout the day, I continued to ask that question and, with only one exception, the answer was the same.[25]

By 7:30 a.m. over 500 people were in line and it was not until almost midnight that the polling place closed. Originally the polls were to close at 8:00 p.m., but because of the huge turnout and the slowness of the process, the Electoral Council decreed that no polling place should close until the last person in line had the opportunity to vote.

As a foreign journalist, I had received an invitation from the Office of the President to see Chávez vote. This was to take place in a school in the *23 de Enero* area close to the presidential palace. Arriving there, I decided to stay outside the building and observe the people, rather than enter.

In the midst of enthusiastic shouts from the bystanders, the presidential motorcade approached. The first black escort vehicle passed us. Then I sensed an awed silence among those standing near me: Chávez was the driver of the next vehicle. With window lowered, he smiled at the people next to me and waved with his left hand. "Chávez was driving the car!" was the gasp that I heard repeated—not something one expects of a president.

That was about midday. I continued to visit with people throughout the day and by midnight was ready to go to bed. I fell asleep but was awakened by the telephone. I was once again invited by the Office of the President to go to the presidential palace where Chávez would be speaking. Exhausted and miles away from the palace I decided not to go and went back to sleep.

Shortly after 3:00 a.m. I was awake again watching television. When they announced at about 3:30 a.m. that Chávez had won the referendum, only the government station carried the news. The commercial channels continued with their regular programming. At 3:35 they started to borrow the broadcast from the government channel showing people celebrating in front of the presidential palace, and then they began to cover Chávez when he spoke.

Interestingly, no commercial stations had their own cameras there. But when Chávez finished his remarks, the viewer was almost immediately taken to a press conference of the opposition where all the major channels had their cameras. There, Henry Ramos Allup announced that there had been a "gigantic fraud." It was now early Monday morning. He said that the details would be made public on Tuesday. But the opposition did not present the details on Tuesday. Nor were they ever able to explain away the two-million vote difference.

The Organization of American States and the Carter Center, together with a multitude of international observers, left the country satisfied that the elections had been clean. The opposition went away angry. But one thing was clearly shown by this democratic process: the opposition was not the majority.

The Actresses and Actors

A Hero, A Ghost

The most important actor in recent Venezuelan history is a person who lived two hundred years ago, Simón Bolívar. To many Venezuelans he is a hero, almost a holy man, probably sitting at the right hand of Jesus Christ in heaven. To others he is a ghost, a frightening spirit, who haunts them day after day after day.

It was quite by accident that I learned anything about Simón Bolívar before coming to Venezuela.

One day when I was in about seventh grade, I was thumbing through the last pages of a social studies book. We never got to the last chapters of any book before the school year ended, so I wanted to see what material we wouldn't cover that year. In the last chapter, I saw a drawing of Simón Bolívar and read that he was to some countries in South America what George Washington was to the United States. That's the only thing that I remember hearing about him before 1985.

Even during the first six months of 1985, which I spent in language school in Bolivia, I didn't hear much mention of him. And yet the country was named after him.

But when I settled in Caracas, I soon learned that he was a very important figure in Venezuela. Paintings of him were everywhere, not only in post offices and schoolrooms, but even in people's living rooms. I would see homemade altars with paintings of him. There were small cards, similar to the holy cards of saints that I knew as child, with his figure on them.

When I think of George Washington, I picture him in the boat crossing the Delaware River, but I can't imagine a painting of him on any altar anywhere in the United States, and I would be surprised to see him in someone's living room.

Then I heard a popular song that began, "Venezuela, my beloved fatherland, which Simón Bolívar liberated." Nothing surprising there, but later in the song it says that some people consider Bolívar a second Jesus Christ! No, I quickly learned, Simón Bolívar was not George Washington.

In the 1980s, Liberation Theology was still at the forefront, but a missionary priest told me that the idea of Jesus as "the liberator" of humanity wasn't an easy concept to put across in Venezuela. The people spoke of only one person as "The Liberator," Simón Bolívar.

At the same time, there were elements of South American history that I didn't understand. The Maryknoll missionary center house was in a part of Caracas called "El Paraíso" (Paradise). It had once been a very wealthy part of Caracas but had become a district of high-rise apartment buildings for the middle class.

Running through the center of the area is Avenida Páez. It is joined to another principal street, Avenida San Martín, by two other avenues, Avenida Santander and Avenida Washington. Páez and Santander both betrayed Bolívar. Santander inspired an assassination attempt against him in 1828. It failed because Bolívar's long-time female friend, Manuela Saenz, saved him. Páez would have been happy if it had succeeded. Then he wouldn't have had to lead the mutiny against Bolívar in 1829. On November 25 of that year, Páez and his followers declared Venezuela separated from Colombia, destroying a great part of Bolívar's dream.

And Washington, who lived before Bolívar, was certainly not more important in Venezuelan history than Bolívar and Francisco de Miranda, who was a contemporary of his. But the Avenida Bolívar and Avenida Miranda that run next to Avenida Washington are much smaller than Avenida Washington. There is even a Plaza Washington—at the end of Avenida Bolívar and Avenida Miranda.

I never paid much attention to these details, although it seemed a bit strange to me that streets would be named after people who were traitors to Simón Bolívar. I couldn't imagine a boulevard in Washington D.C. called "Lee Harvey Oswald" running past a small side street called "John F. Kennedy." It was also strange that the inhabitants of the area seemed to admire Washington (and the United States) more than those who liberated their own country from the Spaniards.

But all of this started to make sense with the discussion of the new constitution. Chávez wanted to rename the country "The Bolivarian Republic of Venezuela," adding the name of Bolívar to its official title. The name of the country had been changed before in recent history. In 1953 it was changed from "The United States of Venezuela" to "The Republic of Venezuela." There had never been any big reaction to that change. But some people didn't like adding the name of Bolívar, and its approval in the new constitution became a point of complaint among Chávez's opponents.

Later on during the coup of April 2002, Pedro Carmona, the self-proclaimed president, ordered that the painting of Bolívar be removed from the room where he would take his oath of office. It was this action more than any other that made me ask: "Who was this Simón Bolívar that Chávez talks about all the time? Why is he so loved by some and so hated by others?"

It is not my intention to present a life of Simón Bolívar, who was born July 24, 1783, and was barely a teenager when George Washington died in 1799. But by the time of his death in 1830, at the age of forty-seven, he had been the principal figure in the liberation of Bolivia, Colombia, Ecuador, Panama, Peru, and Venezuela.

Bolívar was born in Caracas. He died, however, in Colombia. Those ten words, in themselves, say a lot about his life. He died in Colombia because he had become persona non grata in Venezuela. Even in Colombia he wasn't especially welcome. His life had been a constant battle with the elite of that epoch.

He was also leery of the United States. He said, "The United States appears to be destined by Providence to plague Latin America with misery in the name of liberty."

Bolívar had a dream for "The Grand Colombia," which

would encompass Ecuador, Colombia, Panama, and Venezuela. It would be a union that would give those countries strength in the years ahead in their relations with Europe and North America. He also wanted to unite the civilian and military populations. The soldiers were to be of the people, for the people, and with the people. He sought union between the indigenous population, the blacks, and the Creoles. He was against slavery.

Other leaders, such as Santander in Colombia and Páez in Venezuela, did not embrace his dreams with equal fervor. Santander, for example, thought the army should protect the interests of the elite, and slavery was still an important part of the commerce of the day.

As Chávez began his campaign for the presidency, it became clear that he was obsessed with the ideals of Bolívar. In spite of the traditional respect that Venezuelan society had shown for Bolívar, it was probably inevitable that conflict would arise as elite interests would once again be at stake.

One day I noticed a painting by the street artist JR Castillo Arnal. He had included Bolívar, Jesus, Gandhi, and Chávez in the same work. I asked him if he saw Chávez as another Bolívar, Jesus, or Gandhi. He replied in the negative. He said that he put them all there because they all had many enemies and traitors. History was just repeating itself.

The Circles

I have often said that I would like to return to first grade and just color circles. Sister Marie Carmel would give us each a page with six circles on it and beneath each circle was the name of a color. Our task was to fill in the circles with the color indicated, without going outside the lines. In my memory, it was a pleasant and easy task.

In Venezuela, the opposition had a similar fascination with the "Bolivarian Circles." There was, however, only one color for them: blood red.

Soon after becoming president, Chávez issued a call to the people to form such Circles. They were to be study and action groups based on the ideals of Simón Bolívar. Within a couple of years, the opposition would call them "circles of terror." They saw them as violent groups, well armed and ready to someday attack those who lived in the wealthy parts of the city.

Self-defense groups were formed in those areas of the city to fend them off. Neighbors were told not to count on the police in such situations because many of the police were from the barrios. There were actually days when some areas set up barricades for fear of invasion. People were told to prepare hot oil to pour from upstairs windows in case anyone tried to enter their buildings.

The fear was ridiculous, but I know of one barrio dweller who was pleased that it existed. The young man worked part time for a security agency and the other part of the day had his own business installing security devices. He said to me, "Let them go on with their phobias. It gives me more business. I say, 'Don't you think it would be good to install another camera there?' and they say, 'Yes, it probably would be a good idea.'"

I have often said that I have never met a finer group of people than those who lived in the barrio where I lived. Like any other citizens of the country, they wanted work, schools for their children, decent housing, and health care. But those who lived outside the barrios didn't seem to recognize the treasure that was there.

One day I read in an alternative, noncommercial newspaper how the upper classes didn't understand the Bolivarian Circles because they didn't know what happens in the barrios when someone dies. I think the author had a point. Let me describe for you what does happen on such an occasion.

If a person from a barrio dies in a hospital, "vultures" swoop down on the family almost immediately. "Vulture" is the word barrio folk use for employees of the funeral homes who linger around the hospitals waiting for a death and then rush to the survivors to get a contract for the funeral. A distraught family member often signs without understanding what is being signed.

Then the process of getting the needed money begins. As soon as word of the death reaches the barrio, neighbors go around with tin cans, asking for donations to help the family pay the funeral expenses.

I remember one such occasion, the death of a baby. When I went to the family's home for the funeral, the father wasn't there. Neither was the beat-up black mortuary car that would carry the child to the cemetery. "Where's the father?" I asked. "He went to pay off the funeral home. They threatened to put him in jail if he didn't come up with the money." It was not uncommon for funerals to be delayed for this reason. The neighbors simply had to keep taking up a collection, and the family had to call other relatives, pleading for the necessary funds.

When the father finally arrived, I spoke to him for a moment. Since I knew he had used his last bolívar to pay for the funeral, I gave him the equivalent of about twenty dollars so he would have something for his family. Then he or some of the neighborhood children carried the casket to the funeral car. (Both practices were common. I don't remember what happened on that particular occasion.)

When we arrived at the cemetery, a gravedigger accompanied us to look for a gravesite. We climbed a hill, stepping over the tombs of a multitude of persons. Then the digger began his work—unsuccessfully. It seemed that everywhere he dug, there was already a casket. In some places it was not necessary even to try since a part of the casket was protruding from the ground, the earth having been washed away during previous rains.

Finally, he found a spot. The child was buried beneath a few feet of dirt. A friend handed a piece of wood to the father and told him to put the child's name on it. No one seemed to have a writing instrument. Finally, someone located a pencil and the father wrote "J-O-N-A-T-O." He looked at me a bit bewildered and, with tears in his eyes, asked, "Is that how you spell the name?" I said I thought there was an "N" at the end. The plaque was finished. The funeral was over.

Another friend whispered to the father, "You should give something to the gravedigger." The father reached into his pocket and gave the man the only money he had: the bill that I had given him.

What did this have to do with the Bolivarian Circles which were spreading throughout Venezuela and which were heavily criticized by the opposition? Well, the middle and upper economic classes don't have to go through the process just described. There are prearranged funeral plans and gravesites one can buy in advance. And if one still needs some additional funds, there are credit cards.

Barrio people don't have these advantages. They only have one another. That is what the Bolivarian Circles were all about: having and being with one another. They were made up of people organizing so that they could help their communities. Maybe the barrio needed water. Maybe it was electricity, a street, or a playground. The opposition tried to portray them as subversive groups studying how to conduct guerrilla warfare against the wealthy. Their members really didn't care what the wealthy were doing nor were they interested in training for war. They had too much to do in their own barrios.

Were there members who had arms? I am sure there were. But the middle and upper classes also had arms and possibly a greater number per capita because weapons are costly. Their self-defense groups seemed to be much more violent in their intentions than the Circles. In the barrio where I lived, I doubt that more than one person in two hundred had any weapon other than a kitchen knife.

Yes, I am convinced that the upper classes didn't understand the Bolivarian Circles because they didn't know what happens when someone dies in a barrio. It is a shame that they didn't.

In spite of the attention given to the self-defense groups, the wealthy and upper-middle classes were also full of people of good will. If they had only understood barrio life, they too would probably have been in favor of the Circles.

In time the Circles in Venezuela faded away, replaced by other groups such as co-operatives and community councils. But internationally they continue to exist, even in the United States, as support groups for the Venezuelan government. Mention of them, however, probably still disturbs those who never understood them.

The Insect

I have never seen anyone in the United States reading the U.S. Constitution on the subway. I've never noticed anyone walking down the street with a copy of it in their hands. I doubt that most North Americans have ever purchased a copy of it. But in Venezuela, conversations about the constitution are everyday occurrences.

President Chávez often held a tiny copy of it in his hands when he addressed the nation. He called it the *bichito* (insect) because it was so small. But the size of the book had nothing to do with the impact it had on Venezuela as the new century began.

In my opinion, two words are the heart of the document. They pump blood not only into the constitution but also into the body of every Venezuelan, whether they support the government or are among the opposition. Those words are *participatory democracy.*

I never paid much attention to the concept of participatory democracy until a security guard at a city office called it to my attention. He heard that I was a foreign journalist and took advantage of a quiet moment to bend my ear.

He asked me if I knew the difference between representative democracy and participatory democracy. I didn't. Democracy was democracy. From the time I was old enough to vote, my parents insisted that I vote in every election. This meant that every two years I could help elect our U.S. representative, every four years our president, and every six years our senator. Federal judges were beyond my control. I don't think I have ever missed a national election. My immigrant parents and Catholic school teachers taught me well what democracy meant. Or, so I thought.

That, said the security guard, is *representative democracy.* "What we have in Venezuela is *participatory democracy*," and he went on to clarify the matter. I was impressed with his explanation, and he taught me something about democracy that my parents and teachers had not.

I had always had the idea that democracy meant that we had the right to elect our representatives but that, once they had been elected, you had to live with the decision of the electorate until the next election. The only way to get rid of an elected official was by impeachment, and that could happen only if the person had committed some horrible crime.

I didn't know about the forthcoming California recall referendum at the time we had our conversation, but the first election of George W. Bush seemed to be a good current example of what I knew of United States democracy. Once the Supreme Court voted him into office, the nation was stuck with him for the next four years.

But the idea of participatory democracy is more than just referendums. It means that citizens, in addition to having the right to hold their elected officials accountable throughout their tenure, also have the right to be involved in the governing process.

Article 62 reads:

"Every citizen, male or female, has the right to freely participate in public matters, directly or through their representatives.

"The participation of the people in the formation, execution, and control of public matters is the means necessary to accomplish the protagonism that will guarantee their complete development, both as individuals and collectively. It is the obligation of the state to facilitate the most favorable conditions for the practice of this."

In summary, it says that all citizens, not just elected officials, have a right to know what is going on in their country and to determine what is to be done.

Mentioning "all citizens" brought to the forefront a part of the society which had been largely overlooked for five centuries, the native Venezuelan.

Only twenty-five words are written in the Preamble before it recognizes "the heroism and sacrifice of our aborigine ancestors." Only God and Simón Bolívar are mentioned before them. In article 9, Spanish is recognized as the official language of Venezuela, but the languages of the indigenous people are also recognized as official. It is pointed out that they are part of the cultural heritage not only of Venezuela but of all humanity. This group of people, whose blood is present in many Venezuelans, has been denigrated through the years and continues to be looked down upon by many people.[26] As I will point out later, one of Chávez's problems as president is that he is proud of his mestizo blood.

But it is not just the indigenous people who are recognized. Women also are given status equal to men's. This is not easy in Spanish. In Mexico I heard a woman singer conclude her concert by saying, "Gracias, amigos." I said to a friend, "Chávez would never say that. He would have said, 'Gracias, amigas y amigos.'" The constitution uses similar wording. For example, it never speaks of the *presidente* without talking about the *presidenta* also, clearly recognizing that possibility in the future.

When one thinks about the lengthy struggle within the Roman Catholic Church over the use of inclusive language in the liturgy, it is amazing how quickly the constitutional assembly of a country could do it.

Two logical developments of participatory democracy were the idea of the referendum, which I have already mentioned, and the right to overthrow any government which does not respect democratic principles and values or which violates human rights (Article 350). The opposition claimed that this second right justified the coup in April 2002. The problem is that the article says that "the people of Venezuela" have the right. What happened was that a small segment of the society interpreted the constitution to their liking and considered themselves "the people." A better manifestation of this right was when the hundreds of thousands poured into the streets to overthrow the self-proclaimed president, Pedro Carmona.

The other idea, that of the referendum, was seen as too little and too late for the opposition. It provided the possibility for a recall of Chávez after he had served half his term, in August 2003. Since the opposition could not wait for that day, there was the attempted coup, the two-month strike, and the sabotage of the petroleum industry—all in an attempt to oust Chávez before that time. When all else failed, the opposition rallied in an attempt to depose him legally.

It is too early to tell what ramifications the concept of participatory democracy in the Venezuelan Constitution will have in the future, not only in Venezuela but throughout the world. As I write this, Bolivia is in the process of preparing for a constitutional convention. Will it include participatory democracy? I hope so.

And, although this might be considered political heresy or blasphemy to some in the United States, as nations revise and develop new constitutions I wonder if the time has not come for the U.S. to do the same.

Angels and Shepherds

Some of my Christmases in Venezuela have not been particularly happy ones. My first Christmas was so different that it left at least a small scar and a bit of fear for all future ones. Celebrating Christmas with sewage running a few feet from your home isn't the same as in Cheyenne, Wyoming, with snowflakes falling from the sky.

There was the Christmas when a child said to me, "You know, everyone here has been sick. My father told me that even the Baby Jesus was sick, and that's why he couldn't bring me any presents."

Another time I asked a little boy if he had received any presents for Christmas, expecting that he would tell me about them. He simply replied, "No."

For years I have prepared my own Christmas cards. I often write stories or poems to share with my family and friends. But I have avoided telling the Nueva Tacagua Christmas stories. Now I think they are important to relate, because the reality for many of my neighbors has dramatically changed.

And while Simón Bolívar, the Constitution, and the Bolivarian Circles were constantly in the news in one way or another, the real force supporting the government was the "little people." Angélica would be a good example.

One Christmas Eve, before I had ever heard the name of Hugo Chávez, I was visiting families. I stopped for a moment at the home of Angélica. She told me she was taking care of a little baby who was sick and wondered if I could do her a favor. That afternoon she had gone with the baby's mother to see a doctor who had given them a prescription for medicine. The doctor's advice was free. The medicine was not, and they didn't have enough money to buy it. Her question was: could I get it for her?

It was probably about 9 p.m. and I asked her if she needed it right away. No, in the morning would be ok.

I assisted at midnight Mass in a neighboring barrio and then shared a meal with the local priest and the religious sisters. When I returned to my neighborhood at about 2 a.m., some young people stopped me. "Charlie, a baby just died." "Where?" I asked. "In Angélica's house."

Not long after I arrived at the cardboard-and-tin shack, the police arrived also. "Where is the mother?" one asked. She wasn't there. "That's why babies die! The mothers don't take care of them!"

He never asked where the father was nor why the mother wasn't present. I would guess that she was working in a bar. Maybe she was a prostitute. I suppose she was trying to get some money for the child's medicine. To say that she was responsible for the child's death was out of order. The mother had entrusted the child to a responsible friend. However, it is not the custom to tell policemen to shut up, and so I restrained myself.

I also remember that when the policemen finally did leave, they had a flat tire on their Jeep and no jack to raise the vehicle. It was not easy for me to share mine, but the Christmas air must have caused me to be kind to them.

When I returned to my shack, I couldn't help but reflect on the incident. Two thousand years ago, it is reported that angels announced to shepherds and to the world the birth of a child. After two centuries of "civilization," a woman with the name of an angel had to announce to the world the death of a child.

Three years ago, on Ash Wednesday, Angélica was working in Caracas. She had a job as a cook in a hospital. Someone called her. The message was simple: her house and all her belongings had just burned to the ground.

A working mother had locked her children into one of the adjoining shacks. They played with matches and about twenty homes were totally destroyed. Fortunately, no one died or was injured in the incident.

That Ash Wednesday, as others were entering Roman

Catholic churches to receive ashes on their foreheads, Angélica was walking among them.

I returned to my old neighborhood the next day to be with the people. I saw Angélica and asked her if there was anything she needed. No, she replied, the Chávez government was taking care of the people very well. Temporarily, each family had their own apartment in a zone called *Ciudadela*, "little city." The apartments were furnished, and doctors were even available to attend to their needs—an incredible difference from the treatment they had received under previous governments.

Eventually Angélica was given a new apartment. She's thrilled with it. Unfortunately the contractor left without finishing all the details such as laying tile and putting up doors inside. A sad sign that even this government is still fighting corruption. But it is far superior to the attention other governments have given her for the past twenty years that I have known her. She will have to pay for it over the course of years, and I know she will. She has always worked hard, even when she was babysitting that Christmas Eve many years ago and as she still does today. Soon a train will run from her area to Caracas, and it will be easier to get a job.

Today in Nueva Tacagua there are two Cuban doctors who meet their patients in a Pentecostal church less than forty yards from where Angélica lived. They live close by and they have medicines. What a contrast to that Christmas Eve when the baby died.

It was people like Angélica who walked miles to the presidential palace when Chávez was kidnapped on April 11, 2002, demanding his return. It was people like Angelica who stood in line for hours to vote in favor of Chávez during the recall referendum on August 15, 2004.

I now enjoy telling my Christmas story about Angélica to friends because there was something of Christmas joy in the days following those two events. But on these occasions it wasn't angels from on high announcing to the world the birth of a savior. It was more like shepherds (although some had names like Angelica) who were proclaiming their love for someone whom they also considered to be a savior.

The Rest of the Cast (or the Caste)

Reading the national and international press before the April 2002 coup, one might have had the impression that the only supporter Chávez had was himself. Cabinet officers had abandoned him. His wife had left him. Nobody liked him.

After the coup, not much changed in the reporting although the impression was given that he did have some support within the poor barrios, especially among the more violent sectors.

The list of his opponents was long: big business, labor, the Catholic Church, nongovernmental organizations, the petroleum workers, the armed forces. Add to that the United States government and business sectors, and one had to wonder how he could possibly stay in power.

But naming the Catholic Church didn't mean that all Catholics were against the government, although many of the hierarchy clearly were. Saying that some generals and admirals in the armed forces weren't happy with having a former lieutenant colonel as president didn't mean that all the troops (most of whom were from the barrios) shared their feelings.

In the following chapters I will look at some of the opposition actors and try to understand why they reacted to the Chávez government as they did.

Jingo Bells

In January 1959 I began to study philosophy at St. Thomas Seminary College in Denver. For the next two-and-a-half years my job was to learn what the great thinkers of history had to say about life. I studied Aristotle and Plato. I even learned how to pronounce Descartes's name correctly. But there evidently wasn't enough time in those years to look at a few thinkers who might also have been worth considering, such as Marx, Lenin, Hegel.

On January 1, 1959, the cruel Cuban dictator, Fulgencio Batista, fled his country, and Fidel Castro began a triumphal march to Havana. Socialism, Communism, Marxism were ideas that we had never touched upon, and yet they were ideas that were touching my peers in other parts of the world.

We led a sheltered life in the seminary. Newspapers and magazines were prohibited in our rooms. We could read them only in the library. Radios were forbidden, too, and we could watch television only between 7:00 and 7:30 p.m., our evening recreation time. I suppose I can excuse the students for not taking a more active interest in current philosophical ideas. Most of us found the old ones boring. Why should we think the new ones any different?

But I don't believe we should forgive our professors so easily. Their job was to prepare priests for the second half of the twentieth century, not for the Middle Ages. (Fortunately, the Second Vatican Council was about to happen, and theologically we were not so ignorant.)

I mention this because I think something similar will happen in other parts of the world if students do not consider the mass media in Venezuela. I believe that any school of journalism or mass communication that does not study what happened here in the beginning of the twenty-first century will be failing in its responsibility to the students.

"Jingo journalism" is the term used to describe the reporting done during the Spanish-American War at the end of the nineteenth century. The United States' commercial media went overboard in their patriotism. I have no idea what term will be used to describe what happened in Venezuela in the past few years when the media went beyond reasonable limits in their loyalty to the ruling classes. The media were so strongly biased against the president, both in their reporting and their editorials, as well as nationally and internationally, that one barrio priest commented, "If the press is the lifeblood of democracy, Venezuela needs a transfusion."

A whole book could be written on this subject, but I will give just a few examples.

When Chávez won the 1998 elections, the traditional parties were devastated. The electorate had trounced them. Then, when the new constitution (Article 67) said that government funds could not be used for political parties, their main supply of money was cut off.

Among those trying to fill this gap were the mass media. The newspapers, television channels, and radio stations began to act as if they were opposition political parties. It soon became apparent that there was no objective reporting, and President Chávez often complained about this. The media (and especially the owners of the mass media channels) portrayed his complaints as oppression. They ran around the world denouncing the government to international press groups, largely controlled by those who owned the media.

For forty years there had been various kinds of censorship exercised by Venezuelan governments without open complaint. But with Chávez, even before he was elected, the media moguls were crying censorship. That it never happened after he was elected didn't matter. They went on denouncing it—even though it didn't exist.

Their antagonism grew and reached a climax during the April 2002 coup. As I have already mentioned, after celebrating the takeover by the Carmona opposition, the commercial media stopped giving any news when it seemed that Chávez was still alive and was returning to take back the presidency. This type of action would seem to violate every basic norm of good journalism. After it occurred, it should have called for a serious rectification on the part of the media. That didn't happen. The reporting got worse.

One example would be the coverage of two demonstrations in October 2002. On the 11th there was a massive march by the opposition. Hundreds of thousands participated and all the major commercial television stations covered it continuously during the day. The next day the daily newspaper, *El Universal,* had front-page coverage in color, and articles about the demonstration dominated the newspaper.

On October 13, there was a demonstration in favor of the government. Again, hundreds of thousands participated. It would be impossible to say if there were more or fewer than on the 11th. On this day, however, there was no coverage of the event by the major commercial channels. The next day, *El Universal* showed one small picture of a tired, smiling woman sitting on a curb holding a homemade sign. It read, "Hungry and unemployed but I will stick with Chávez to the end." The principal front-page headline that day was about baseball.

Then came the so-called "strike" which began on December 2, 2002. For the next two months, the principal newspapers, television channels, and radio stations accepted no commercial advertising. (Imagine in the United States *The New York Times, Wall Street Journal,* ABC, NBC, CBS, and CNN with no advertisements or commercials for two months.) The only television commercials were antigovernment propaganda, and they were being broadcast constantly. Even when children's programming appeared, it was interrupted with antigovernment spots.

And the spots were vicious. One said that there was room in Venezuela for everyone "except you," referring to the president. Another had a child pitching a baseball to an adult and striking him out. It was clear who the adult was as he walked away from the home plate. Chávez is known for his love of baseball, not only as a fan but as a participant.

In addition, all other programming was antigovernment. It was a twenty-four-hour barrage of one-sided propaganda. The news reporting was so biased it seemed to be more like editorial writing than news reporting.

From the time I was in elementary school, I had learned that a news story should try to be objective and should address the questions Who? What? Why? When? Where? and How? I also believed that journalism was a noble profession. What had gone wrong?

On the part of the owners of the media, the answer seemed clear: there were moneyed interests involved. Chávez seemed to be a threat to the elite who had dominated the country for decades and they, as well as their top staff, were a part of that group.

But what about the young reporters? I once heard that everyone is liberal and radical in their youth. It is in middle age that one becomes conservative or even reactionary. Why did they see things so differently than I did? Reflecting on this situation, I came up with an answer. If they were twenty-five in 2002, they were only about twelve in 1989. They didn't have the memories that I had of Venezuela, of hundreds being shot down on the streets and buried in garbage bags. Being college-educated in Venezuela generally means being from the middle or upper classes. Even if they were over 25, they probably didn't have all the memories that barrio dwellers had. I had a friend who was a professor in the school of communication of the Catholic University Andrés Bello. He often commented on the lack of social awareness of his upper-class students whose only desire in the field of communication was to make money.

This second reason might also explain why their older mentors in the commercial mass media didn't seem to know what life was like back then. Otherwise, they must have been suffering from serious cases of amnesia. I often heard them and their peers saying after the election of Chávez, "We've never had a situation this bad in Venezuela." Oh?

I have copies of newspapers from 1992 with whole pages blank because the material had been censored. That was during the government of Carlos Andrés Pérez. There were times when whole editions were confiscated by the government. Jaime Lusinchi, Pérez's predecessor, had another way of manipulating the news. The newspapers needed to import the newsprint, but only those who would not print anything against Lusinchi could receive dollars at a preferential exchange rate, making it impossible for them to stay in business if they opposed him. PROVEA has lists of attacks on journalists through the years before Chávez was elected.

I can say the following without fear of being contradicted: there was not one word against Chávez that couldn't be printed or spoken from the beginning of his presidency until the writing of this book. It is a shame that the same cannot be said about the media's treatment of words favorable to the government.

But a very positive development came from all of this. Alternative newspapers, radio stations, and television channels began to multiply and even had the encouragement of the government. The newspapers were often started by people with little journalistic expertise but lots of dedication. They would gather what money they could to print the first edition. Then, after selling it on the streets, they would use that money to help them put out another.

The radio stations came into being in a similar manner. They were neighborhood stations and often used homemade equipment. I was familiar with Radio Catia Libre (Radio Free Catia). During the coup it was raided. It was not on the air at the time, and only a teenager with no particular political affiliation was in the building. He was handcuffed and driven around the area by the police for several hours before being released. (This is called *ruleteo*. It is the common name for an illegal police procedure in Venezuela which involves putting a person in a vehicle, driving him around without a definite destination while he is harassed, interrogated, and beaten.) I was told that the youth, with aspirations of working in radio someday, never returned to Radio Catia Libre out of fear.

After the coup, I visited Radio Perola (Radio Pots and Pans) in another part of Caracas. It operated out of the bedroom of someone's apartment and broadcast from about 6 a.m. to 11 p.m., totally through the work of volunteers.

When people were to be interviewed, they were asked not to come more than ten minutes beforehand because there was no place for them to wait other than the small living room of the apartment. The antenna sticking out of the window brought to my mind the rabbit ears used when television first appeared in the United States, and yet Radio Perola was the most listened-to station in the area.

They went off the air when the April 2002 coup was happening and hid their simple equipment. When the police came they didn't find anyone or anything. But they continued their search and eventually arrested Nicolás Rivera Muentes. At the time, Nicolás was 26 years old and the father of three children (four-year-old twins and a two-year-old). His family lived in the working-class neighborhood of Caricuao, where he was employed as a supervisor of children in care of the National Institute of Children (INAM).

Nicolás was also a director of Radio Perola, and as one of the station's announcers he had a music program called SOLO SALSA (Only Salsa).

At 9 p.m. on April 12, the day that Mr. Carmona declared himself president of Venezuela, the police (the PTJ) raided the INAM where Nicolás worked, forced him into a vehicle, and drove him around the area for several hours. His captors beat Nicolás continually while he was asked for information about the radio equipment and the other volunteers at the station.

He was taken to his home at 1 a.m. on April 13. The house was raided and, in the presence of his father, mother, wife, brothers (ages 25, 15, and 15), brother-in-law, and children, Nicolás was beaten for approximately two hours. Afterwards, he was again "ruleteado" and threatened with death if he didn't take them to the radio transmitter. At one moment he was taken out of the vehicle, beaten, kicked, and pistol-whipped.

He was then taken to the headquarters of the PTJ and beaten again. He was held there without food or water until April 14, when the coup had failed. He had been charged with complicity in an intentional homicide—the charge was thrown out by another judge, and he was released.

All of this information was taken from an appeal made to the InterAmerican Commission of Human Rights of the Organization of American States, May 10, 2002.

These actions were also made known to the local police. Not receiving any response, Nicolás went to the PTJ on June 28, accompanied by his wife and some friends. He was arrested again for supposedly appearing in a video shooting a weapon, and was then imprisoned as a common criminal. Friends told me he carried a tape recorder with him that day.

I visited with Nicolás's family one day. His wife told me how, on the night of April 12-13, the police handcuffed her also and beat her in front of the children. At one moment she noticed a policeman taking some bullets from his pocket. These were later "found" by the police among her children's clothing. The police threatened to arrest her also and take her children away from her. As they were taking her out of the crying children's room, her plea to her mother-in-law and sister-in-law was, "Don't let them take the children."

Other members of the family were also handcuffed, and Nicolás's father pulled by his hair.

When I visited with the family, Nicolás's mother had just

returned from talking to a government human rights official. One of her children asked her, "Did you cry, Mom?" She just looked at him. There was no need to reply.

She told me that Nicolás had always been a dreamer, hoping for a better and more just world. She was also concerned about her other children, especially the boys, who continued to be volunteers with Radio Perola. While we were conversing, one of the boys shook my hand and went out the door.

Having finished our conversation and while walking in the direction of the bus stop, a friend turned on his portable radio. "Good afternoon and welcome again to SOLO SALSA. This is your host, Victor Hugo Rivera." It was a voice I had heard moments before. Now it was coming over Radio Perola. It was Nicolás's teen-age brother. His brother was in prison. His program and ideals were not.

Nicolás was eventually released from prison in the spring of 2003.

Whenever I read in the press that Chávez was a "dictator" and about the so-called "oppression of the press," it would make me angry. What dictator has ever encouraged neighborhood presses and radio stations? What did happen in fact, during the coup, was the violation of the press's freedom. During those few hours that Carmona was in power, several radio stations were raided and their participants were hunted. But the *jingo-bell* commercial press of Venezuela never spoke about this.

Money

About a year after the coup, a taxi driver shared a story with me. I cannot confirm the truthfulness of what he said, but I think it is important to repeat it, and hopefully the reader will find it as interesting as I did. I will put it in his words as I remember them.

"One day I had two generals as passengers from the airport to Caracas. One of them told me that he had been close to Chávez since the 1992 coup attempt. He said that when Chávez was campaigning for the presidency, many of the big business people had given him money for his campaign. They had done their own surveys and in spite of what the media were saying, they knew that Chávez was going to win the election.

"When the election was over, Chávez was invited to a luxurious meal with some of these people and their wives. The general was invited also. It was a wonderful evening with lots of praise for the new president. At the end of the meal, the men invited Chávez to go into an adjoining room. There they presented to the new president, who had not yet taken office, a list of people they wanted appointed to important government posts. Chávez looked at the list and replied, 'I thank you for your suggestions, but I am now president of Venezuela, and I have already decided who I would like to fill these posts. I am sorry but none of the people I have chosen are on this list. Gentlemen, I do have another commitment this evening, so I must be going.' He left the meeting."

As I stated, I have no way of confirming the accuracy of this story, but it did bring to mind an article which had appeared in *The New York Times* a year before about Gustavo Cisneros, Venezuela's wealthiest citizen and the second wealthiest in Latin America. The article said:

"When it became apparent in 1998 that Mr. Chávez... would be elected president, Mr. Cisneros and other influential businessmen in Venezuela supported him and sought to influence him....

"Their support for Mr. Chávez eroded, however, after the president made clear that he planned to pursue fundamental changes in Venezuela to try to redistribute wealth in the country, where 80 percent of the population lives in poverty. Mr. Chávez's speeches often had references to 'squalid oligarchs' bent on preserving their upper-class privileges."[27]

In this article, the author explains some of the sources of Cisneros's wealth, including his investment in the mass media. At the time Cisneros Group was the largest shareholder in Univision which owned 18 stations in the United States. It also distributed yearly over 19,000 hours of programming "to 40 million households in 21 countries on three continents."

That statement in itself should give some idea of the power of this opponent of Hugo Chávez, even without mentioning any of his other investments. It is also well known that he is a friend of George H. W. Bush, who has joined Cisneros for fishing trips in Venezuela.

My contact with Gustavo Cisneros would have been only as a consumer of Pepsi-Cola. My association with Pepsi in some ways was a strange relationship since I didn't have much choice in the matter.

When I first arrived in Venezuela in 1985, it was almost impossible to buy a Coke. The reason was that since the 1940's the Cisneros family had the Pepsi-Cola franchise and for some reason Coca-Cola was never able to get a strong footing in Venezuela. That is, until 1996.

In my memory, it took only about a week and suddenly there was no Pepsi-Cola available. The Cisneros family had decided to change to Coca-Cola. They also decided that all of Venezuela should change with them. The Pepsi blue disappeared and Coca-Cola red quickly dominated the fronts of bakeries, grocery stores, liquor outlets, and the sides of a whole fleet of delivery trucks. Fast-food franchises that had exclusive contracts with Pepsi had to fly the product in from Miami.

Eventually another powerful family, the Mendozas, obtained the Pepsi bottling operation for Venezuela. Since then, prices for soft drinks have dropped. It was always a sore point for me that barrio dwellers had to pay higher prices for soft drinks than people in the United States. Lack of clean water in some ways forced them to drink those products. I also knew that it only took a few drops of syrup and carbonated water to produce them, and the high prices in Venezuela in no way seemed justified. I would have had no problem with the price if the Venezuelan worker received a salary similar to his U.S. counterpart in a bottling plant. But the minimum hourly wage in the United States was about the same as the minimum daily salary for a Venezuelan.

The matter of soft drinks reached a comic climax in Venezuela during the December 2002-January 2003 "strike" when none were available. On January 17, General Acosta Carles led a group of National Guardsmen in a raid on a Coca-Cola warehouse in the state of Carabobo, followed by a similar one at Pepsi-Cola. The buildings were full. It was a media event during which the general, standing in front of skyscrapers of soft drinks, deliberately burped after drinking one.

Meanwhile, outside, a group of women in opposition to the government gathered to defend the Coca-Cola warehouse. Dressed in black t-shirts and slacks, they rushed the National Guardsmen. The soldiers resisted and also fired tear gas. At least one woman fell to the ground and was pulled away from the scene by supporters.

The whole scene reminded me of a professional wrestling match, but what surprised me was when a reporter asked the general if Coca-Cola was a product of prime necessity for the population, and he affirmed that it was.

Legally, I don't know if it was classified as such. But the fact that companies such as Coca-Cola and Pepsi-Cola would keep their product off the market for over a month to help oust a democratically elected government is worthy of reflection.

The taxi driver I told about at the beginning of this chapter spoke of the Cisneros and the Mendozas. He also mentioned several other names with which I was not familiar and which I do not now remember.

Was his story true? Was it accurate? I have no way of knowing. Could it have happened? I think it could have.

John L. Lewis, Shivering

The principal spokesman for the labor movement in Venezuela was Carlos Ortega, president of the CTV. However, Ortega became so closely identified with big business and their ideals that it was hard to separate him from them. He was really more a spokesman for big business than for the worker.

The "strikes" he called were never really strikes but "lockouts." Big business shut down their factories, and the workers had no choice but to stay home from work. Executives led the 2002-2003 petroleum industry strike, not the rank and file. There were even moments when the leaders of the big business association, FEDECAMARAS, were annoyed by his actions. Ortega, supposedly a labor leader, appeared to be making decisions for them and was stealing the spotlight from them.

When Ortega held his press conferences in December 2002 and January 2003, he was always in a five-star hotel where the only working-class people were those who cleaned the rooms, waited on tables, and did the maintenance. When Ortega addressed the massive rallies of the opposition, he was addressing white people wearing designer clothing and sunglasses. But when Chávez conducted his Sunday *Aló Presidente* program, he was always in the barrio or in places where the working class was.

A sore point in the relations between the government and the CTV was that Chávez never wanted to recognize Ortega as its legitimate president. Legally, the National Electoral Council (the CNE) was the body to supervise the elections of the CTV. But half of the ballots never arrived to be checked. The CTV didn't recognize the authority of the CNE, and Carlos Ortega, with the help of the media, was recognized as the leader of the CTV.

The CTV always had close ties to the AD party and was really the only remnant of the party that still had massive funds and continued to function after the searing defeat of the 1998 elections. When Ortega sought asylum in the Costa Rican embassy and was about to leave Venezuela, the *ADecos* made him honorary president of their party.

As a United States citizen, I felt personal shame in knowing that the AFL-CIO was aiding the CTV financially. If John L. Lewis, the great leader of the labor movement in the U.S., had been alive I think he would have shivered at the coldness both the AFL-CIO and the CTV showed toward the needs of the ordinary Venezuelan worker.

After the prolonged "strike" ended in failure in February 2003, a split occurred in the CTV. Those leading the breakaway group were accused of being identified with the government. What the CTV leaders didn't seem to realize was that there was a need for a labor union that was identified with the workers.

Combat Boots

Three blocks from the Caracas cathedral the street artist I mentioned before, JR (José) Castillo Arnal, displayed his works. I first noticed them a few weeks after the April 2002 coup. Some were huge paintings, measuring over six feet in length.

One of them portrayed five Catholic bishops sitting at a table. They were dressed in full hierarchical attire but their robes didn't cover the combat boots they were wearing. I recognized two of the bishops—Cardinal Ignacio Velasco, the archbishop of Caracas, and Baltazar Porras, the president of the Venezuelan Bishops' Conference. But I didn't recognize the bishop sitting between them, sporting camouflage pants. I asked José the name of that bishop. He replied that it was the United States ambassador to Venezuela, John Maisto, dressed as a bishop.

I had been impressed that Mr. Castillo could paint the picture so quickly after the coup. But it turned out that he had painted it two years before when John Maisto was the ambassador. Castillo seemed to have been a prophet in light of the role that the Cardinal would play in the coup events. If I had been the archbishop passing the painting that day, I think I would have bowed my head in shame.

One year later, the daily newspaper *Ultimas Noticias* reported that the code name used for the Cardinal during the preparations for the coup was "Zamuro Negro" (Black Vulture).

Now if I had been the archbishop, I think I would have cried upon seeing those words in print. Although only a code name, they seemed insulting to me. But even worse should have been the knowledge that many faithful Catholics would have considered the title appropriate for him, and for some of his fellow bishops as well.

When Cardinal Velasco died in July 2003, I went to the cathedral to view his body, the first and only time I ever saw him. Surrounding Plaza Bolívar in front of the church there was a heavy presence of National Guardsmen with gas masks hanging from their arms or necks. In front of the cathedral, the Metropolitan Police had their shields and were prepared for any rioting that might occur.

I only had about a ten-minute wait to enter the Cathedral, but as I stood in line a woman passed in the opposite direction. In a loud voice she was saying, "He was a rat! He was an assassin!" A woman behind me remarked, "I guess everyone is entitled to their own opinion."

What could have provoked such a situation and a remark like that about the highest-ranking member of the Catholic clergy in Venezuela? There had been a whole series of events, not the least of which were the showing of videos and photos of the moment when the dictator, Carmona, declared himself president. The Cardinal appeared in the front row on Carmona's right. They also showed him smiling.

The Cardinal was the first to sign his name after the dictatorial decrees were read. He later denied that he signed the decrees and said that he only signed a "blank" paper. He also said that he signed it in order to avoid disturbances in the group that was there cheering Carmona.

The editor of *Ultimas Noticias* was not only able to write that the Cardinal did sign the decrees, but was even able to point out that his signature was immediately after that of Carmona and before other names, which he listed in order.

In some ways it really didn't matter what he signed. He signed. It was a disturbing day for many Catholics. A young barrio woman asked me, "Do you think the Pope will punish him for what he did?" The idea was unthinkable to me, and the question surprised me. I finally replied, "I don't think so," and felt personal pain as a Catholic in saying the words.

I knew Cardinal Velasco's predecessor, Cardinal José Alí Lebrún, and often felt that the whole history of these recent years would have been different if he were still alive. Cardinal Lebrún had visited Nueva Tacagua on a few occasions, and we had had several meetings in his office. I felt he was a conciliator. On the other hand, using direct confrontation, some of the Catholic hierarchy had engaged in a running battle with Chávez since before his election. Cardinal Velasco became a part of that group.

When the horrible landslides of 1999 occurred, the Cardinal said that it was God's punishment of the people for what they had done. Many interpreted his remarks as referring to the new constitution which was approved that same day.

But his statement on January 23, 2002, about ten weeks before the Carmona coup, needed no interpretation. It was clearly in opposition to the government. On that day two demonstrations were to be held: one against the government and the other in favor. January 23 is the date when the dictator, Pérez Jiménez, was overthrown in 1958. There is a working-class section of Caracas that bears the name El 23 de Enero (the 23rd of January), and a Mass was celebrated in one of its parish churches early in the morning. President Chávez was present for the Mass with his wife, the vice-president, and various other government dignitaries. It was broadcast nationwide on all radio stations and TV channels. This especially perturbed the opposition, which had antigovernment talk shows prepared for the time slot.

Before the day was over, the Cardinal had issued a letter in which he stated that "the group of priests who led the Eucharist...do not represent either the institution nor the majority of the Catholics of Venezuela." He complained that a slogan on the wall behind the altar and things that were said made it a political happening. The slogan was a statement by Archbishop Oscar Romero who had been assassinated in El Salvador in 1980.

The next day, the president's annual reception for the foreign diplomatic corps became another moment of confrontation between the church and the government. In his presentation before the other diplomats, the apostolic nuncio,

Bishop André Dupuy, praised the president for his dynamism and generosity on behalf of the poor, but also warned of the danger of a "radicalization" of the political process here. In his reply, the president defended the priests who had celebrated the Mass and complained that some of the Catholic hierarchy were a "tumor" on the political process.

Two days later the main headline of *El Nacional,* one of the principal opposition newspapers, read, "When the tumor surrounding the President is opened, the stench will reach the end of the world." They were quoting Archbishop Roberto Luckert, a leading spokesperson for the hierarchy.

The following day, a Sunday, a Catholic church supplement in *El Nacional, IGLESIA* (Church) carried photos only of the January 23 opposition march and of Archbishop Baltazar Porras, President of the Bishops' Conference, shaking hands with the editor of *El Nacional.* It also carried a January 11 statement of the Bishops' Conference calling for dialog as the road to peace. However, on Monday, the bishops met with Alfredo Peña, the mayor of the greater Caracas area and one of the most outspoken critics of the government. They also decided *not* to meet with the president at a meeting that had been scheduled for the next day.

These events came after three years of tension between the president and the hierarchy. Shortly after his election in December 1998, Chávez had followed the usual tradition of the president by attending the annual meeting of the bishops. Then he stopped attending.

There were also problems with the subsidies of the Catholic Church. The Catholic Church in Venezuela annually submits a budget to the government. For some reason, it had been reduced during the Caldera government. Also the government sometimes provided housing, cars, and chauffeurs for the bishops. Chávez seemed to feel other religions should also benefit from government funds if the Catholic Church did.

Chávez often used strong language and seemed closed to his opponents and uncompromising. But the hierarchy was not always sociable and gentle, either. The July 29, 2001, issue of *IGLESIA* was headlined with a quotation from the president of the Venezuelan Bishops' Conference, Archbishop Baltazar Porras: "POWER is the new IDOL in Venezuela." The "O" of POWER was extra large and had a photograph of the president in the center.

In addition, *IGLESIA* had among its supporters three of the Caracas television stations and *El Nacional*, all known to be in opposition to the government.

In 2001, the bishops gave the Bishop Pellin Award to the television station most confrontational with the government. One political leader supporting the government said that the Church seemed to be an opposition party.

Following the coup, I had a meeting with Bishop Ubaldo Santana, second vice-president of the Bishops' Conference at the time, regarding the attitude of the bishops. Bishop Santana often visited Nueva Tacagua, and I have great respect for him. He said that it was important to look at the official statements of the Conference and not at the actions of any individual bishop. Theoretically that sounds nice, but it should be noted that a few days after the bishops issued their January 2002 statement on dialog, they refused to meet with President Chávez. He also mentioned that the publication *IGLESIA* was the work of an individual priest and shouldn't be seen as representing the hierarchy. Yet the priest had been rector of the Venezuelan seminary in Rome. Surely the bishops could have controlled his actions if they had wanted to do so.

Finally, one of the most confrontational bishops was Archbishop Baltazar Porras, the president of the Bishops' Conference. When the elections for a new Conference president were held after the April coup, he was re-elected. The bishops seemed to reflect the attitude of the opposition in general: we did no wrong. Why should we have to give an inch? Clearly more than pious statements were needed for the Church to be seen as representing all sectors of the population.

In addition to the response of the bishops, some mention should also be made of the Jesuits. The Jesuit magazine *SIC* had been recognized through the years as a responsible critic of all the governments. It was also very heavy in its criticism of this one. However, it listed as its directress a committed Catholic laywomen with ties to the COPEI party that had been badly beaten by Chávez. This does not mean that her leadership necessarily interfered with the impartiality of the magazine, but it would seem to have been of questionable value in a time of conflict.

There is also a photo of Luis Ugalde that will forever haunt them. Ugalde was rector of the Catholic University Andrés Bello in Caracas and former superior of the Jesuits in Venezuela. On March 6, 2002, just a few weeks before the coup, there were front-page photos of Ugalde holding hands high in the air with Pedro Carmona and Carlos Ortega. As a representative of the bishops, he was with them issuing a statement on how the country could be governed while in transition—meaning without Chávez. Five weeks later Carmona showed himself to be a dictator. After his fall, Ortega took the reins as opposition spokesperson.

A fellow Jesuit of Ugalde told me after the coup that Ugalde did not regret the meeting because he was able to get recognition of the poor worked into the statement. I doubt many barrio people noticed that recognition considering what they had proclaimed. The front-page photo was unforgettable.

As a Catholic, a former priest, and a friend of some bishops and Jesuits, I found all this confrontation painful. Good criticism of many government actions was necessary, and the bishops and Jesuits were among the most capable of giving such. However, the language and behavior of some members of the hierarchy and clergy clearly identified them with the opposition.

Sadly, the powerful voice the Catholic leaders could have had became only a loud voice.

The Devil's Excrement

Venezuela is one of the world's largest petroleum exporters. The indigenous people knew of the existence of oil and called it the "excrement of the devil." A little commercial extraction was done in the 1800's and more serious production began in 1917. But it was not until December 15, 1922, when a well gushed near Lake Maracaibo, that world attention focused on the oil of Venezuela. For eight days the oil was out of control as hundreds of men tried to open ditches to manage the flow, the only thing they could do.

From that day, Venezuela has been identified with oil, and it soon became a paradise for large oil companies such as the Creole Petroleum Corporation (affiliated with Standard Oil of New Jersey), the Compañia Shell de Venezuela (belonging to the Royal Dutch Company), and the Gulf Oil Corporation. Others such as Sinclair, Mobil, Texaco, Phillips, Chevron, etc. were associated with these.[28]

Through the years, the Venezuelan people benefited little from the exportation of oil as corrupt politicians worked together with the foreign companies to keep their income high and Venezuela's low. At one point the importation tax benefits to the foreign companies were so great that the Minister of Development said it would be better to give the oil away and charge them excise taxes on what they were importing.

In 1976, the oil industry was nationalized without great problems. The oil companies were pleased with the terms.

Enough ancient history. Let us look at the 1990's and the beginning of the new century.

From the start of his presidency, Chávez seemed to be picking a fight with the directors of the national oil company, PDVSA. In one of his first speeches, he said that PDVSA owned more airplanes than any Venezuelan airline. It was common knowledge that the employees of PDVSA were well paid and well treated, but few people knew much more about the company. A taxi driver once commented to me that the parking lot of the PDVSA offices in Caracas looked like the showroom of a new-car dealer.

But it was not only the ordinary person who knew little about PDVSA. The government didn't either. PDVSA became known as a "black box," a "government within the government."

On January 28, 2002, the Comptroller General of Venezuela raised questions about a contract which PDVSA had with Intesa, a U.S.-based company, and its associated company, SAIC (Science Applications International Corporation). High-ranking officials in SAIC included former U.S. military officers and CIA officials, such as General Wayne Downing (who was appointed by President George W. Bush to head the White House Office for Combating Terrorism), General Jasper Welch (who was formerly a coordinator for the National Security Council), and Admiral Bobby Ray Inman (who was the former director of the National Security Agency and deputy director of the CIA). The comptroller's investigations revealed millions of dollars in losses and implicated high-ranking PDVSA officials. On February 13, (the former General) Guaicaipuro Lameda, president of PDVSA, was fired.

In his place, Chávez appointed Gastón Parra Luzardo, a prominent professor and economist who had written extensively about petroleum. He promised that he would rigorously analyze what was happening in PDVSA. He was accompanied by another petroleum expert, Carlos Mendoza Potellá.

On February 25, President Chávez appointed a new board of directors. At this, a protest cry of "meritocracy!" came from within the company. The notion was that PDVSA was being politicized by Chávez, that those who were being appointed knew nothing about the company, and that only those who had worked their way up through the ranks should occupy executive posts within the company.

It sounded logical at the moment, but also contradictory. When General Guaicaipuro Lameda was appointed, he had not worked his way up through the organization and there had been no protest. He had lived happily within the ranks of PDVSA for almost a year. Parra Luzardo, on the other hand, was a petroleum expert. Why the concern?[29]

This appointment, however, gave FEDECAMARAS and the CTV the opportunity to bring the petroleum industry into their efforts to tumble Chávez. Lameda helped organize acts of protest and sabotage.

On April 6, Carlos Ortega of the CTV called for a 24-hour strike to take place on Tuesday, April 9. FEDECAMARAS and the leadership of PDVSA joined in. On Sunday, April 7, President Chávez dismissed thirteen executives of PDVSA and forced the retirement of twelve more. This was done publicly during his weekly *Aló Presidente* radio and TV program.

The strike did not terminate on the 9th. As was previously described, on Thursday, April 11, the march in support of PDVSA ended up at the presidential palace and marked the beginning of the April 2002 coup.

When the president was back in office, he apologized for the way he had dismissed the executives, and they found themselves back in power. A new president was appointed for PDVSA, Alí Rodríquez Araque, who was secretary general of OPEC at that moment.

The appointment of Alí Rodríquez turned out to be a blessing for the government. Leaving the other executives in their positions, however, was a grave error. The plotting against the government continued and led to the second coup, the "economic coup" which began on December 2, 2002.

It was not until after this "strike" that the public began to see what was inside the "black box." The whole nation had been affected during the two months that it lasted. What could have justified such actions on the part of the PDVSA executives and employees?

During the months after the strike, seminars were held throughout the country, giving people information on how PDVSA had been operating. For the first time ever, ordinary people were learning about *their* oil company.

In the 1980s, about 70 percent of the income from petroleum went to the government and 30 percent was used for operating expenses. In the year 2000 only 20 percent went to the government. Operating expenses had consumed the rest. Venezuela was ranked 50th in this regard in comparison with other countries: in Petroecuador 70.7 percent went to the country, in Petroperú 50.3 percent, in Petrobras (of Brazil) 39.9 percent, etc.

For each dollar that PDVSA invested, it received a return of $7.00. Shell was able to produce $14.00, and Texaco and Exxon $13.00 in their companies.

Each employee of PDVSA was producing an average of $777,000 annually. Texaco employees produced $1,900,000 and Exxon employees $1,800,000.

Two months after the strike ended, on April 12, 2003, Alí Rodríquez summed it up in a few words when he said that PDVSA was again producing at full capacity with a 40-percent smaller work force. The efficiency of PDVSA had not been as great as its former executives had said it was.

ADOs

Samuel Moncada, at that time head of the history department of the Central Venezuelan University (UCV) in Caracas, said to me one day, "I think Venezuela is the only country in the world where NGO (nongovernmental organization) means a 'political action group trying to overthrow the government'." He was expressing in different words an opinion that another friend had offered a few weeks before when he asked me, "Charlie, is there any possibility that you could go to the United States and raise funds to form an NGO here *in favor of the government?*"

I had never paid much attention to the term "NGO" before the election of President Chávez. I had neither favorable nor unfavorable feelings toward such organizations. They simply were not a part of my daily life or concern.

In Nueva Tacagua I did have one experience with an NGO from Europe which seemed to me more concerned with the salary of its executives than with really helping people in the underdeveloped world. One bad experience, however, was no reason to judge NGOs in general, and they certainly weren't trying to overthrow any government.

To me, the term "NGO" applied to aid organizations, human rights groups and even extended to groups such as the Girl Scouts and Boy Scouts, the YMCA and the YWCA. But the idea of an NGO whose main purpose seemed to be the overthrow of a democratically elected government didn't fit into my vision of what an NGO was supposed to be.

With the arrival of the new century in Venezuela, however, I found myself cringing whenever I saw the term NGO in the newspaper. After the almost complete fall of the traditional political parties following the 1998 elections and the search for some groups to fill the gap, a variety of NGOs had sprung up. Just as the political parties that began in the late 90s were started by and centered on one person (Irene Saez, IRENE; Salas Römer, PROYECTO VENEZUELA;

Julio Borges, PRIMERO JUSTICIA; Antonio Ledezma, ALIANZA BRAVO PUEBLO; etc.) so did each of these NGOs seem to be led by one person.

The newspapers were replete with articles that mentioned the number of NGOs that were against some government action. It made for good antigovernment publicity both nationally and internationally, but many were just fronts for some person or small group of people who had a gripe with the government. It would also be interesting to find out someday to what extent the CIA was involved in the funding of these in light of similar activities in other Latin American countries.

However, there were groups that had been organized well before 2002 and could have been properly considered as NGO's before the Chávez government took power. Some of them also became political action groups of the opposition.

QUEREMOS ELIGIR (We Want to Elect), for example, had been founded by Elías Santana, a person with years of experience in community organizations. It had done good work in promoting direct elections in Venezuela where members of congress had been simply designated by their parties. Seats had been given in accordance with the number of votes the party had received in the presidential elections. The parties filled them with people who had to vote strictly according to the instructions of the leadership of the party or be removed.

But with the election of Chávez, Santana became an organizer and leader of marches and demonstrations against the government and signed a public document in support of the April coup when it happened. That was a strange reaction from someone who headed an organization called "We Want to Elect." When the Coordinadora Democrática was founded, he had been actively involved in it.

The title of the organization also seemed a bit ridiculous after six consecutive and clean elections[30] in which government supporters predominated. Elías Santana was a favorite of the press but no one ever raised the question: "Who elected Elías Santana?"

COFAVIC (The Committee of Family Members of the Victims) is another example. This was an NGO formed after the massacre of February 27, 1989. Its original purpose was to seek justice by identifying and prosecuting those to blame for the killing of innocent victims. But gradually control of the organization fell into the hands of a young lawyer, Liliana Ortega, and the legal thrust became the indemnification of the families.

Ms. Ortega gained international fame with an article that appeared in *TIME* in 1999 listing her as one of Latin America's "Leaders for the New Millennium." In 1997 an international body decided that the family of one of the 1989 victims she was representing was entitled to a thirty-thousand-dollar compensation. Her media efforts after that seemed to focus more on the responsibility of the Chávez government to pay this than on the crime committed during the reign of Carlos Andrés Pérez.

One day I spoke with the father of an eight-year-old who had been killed when the armed forces fired indiscriminately at the building where they lived. Financial indemnification was of little use to him. What money could ever replace his child? It seemed to be a capitalist value rather than a human one. It also seemed to be the concern of COFAVIC, an organization that had lost sight of its original purpose.

In writing this, I do not mean that there is no value in financial remuneration. Indeed, it seems to me to be a matter of justice and a way of holding governments accountable. But when it becomes a publicity instrument to embarrass a government that had nothing to do with the crimes committed, something smells fishy to me.

After the election of Chávez, Liliana Ortega's name became completely identified with the opposition.

Other human rights groups, however, maintained most of the prestige they had had before the election. PROVEA and the Red de Apoyo (The Support Network) seemed to be trying to fulfill their role in evaluating human rights violations wherever they occurred, no matter whether the government or the opposition was responsible. This was possibly because these organizations were group endeavors. They had no single spokesperson, and those within the organizations had differing political opinions.

Another spokesman for the opposition from the NGO sector was Armando Janssens, a Belgian Catholic priest, who formed CESAP[31] many years ago. CESAP was an organization dedicated to the formation of community groups and leaders.

In the late 1980's the Maryknoll Missionaries had a serious falling out with CESAP. The matter centered around a cartoon which was to be printed in one of CESAP's publications. It expressed some sentiments that were seen to be against U.S. policy in Central America, and the editors were told to remove it. The reason: CESAP was receiving funds from an "independent" agency of the United States government, the Inter-American Foundation (IAF).

In another incident, a representative of the Inter-American Foundation visited a women's group. A Maryknoll lay missioner had helped to start the group, but the women were told that she should not be invited to their meeting that day. The lay missioner's house was across the street from the meeting place. When the women questioned CESAP about the reason, they were informed that Maryknoll was too leftist and communist. Maryknoll had actually given funds to CESAP through the years.

Searching the Internet, I discovered that both CESAP and Queremos Eligir had received in recent years hundreds of thousands of dollars from the Inter-American Foundation and from the National Endowment for Democracy (NED). The NED also receives its funding from the United States government. Jeremy Bigwood, an investigative reporter in Washington D.C., did a much more extensive study of the involvement of the U.S. government through groups such as the IAF and the NED. He discovered that millions of dollars had been transferred to opposition groups in Venezuela. Eva Golinger published the results of this investigation in THE CHÁVEZ CODE.[32]

CESAP also wanted to become the clearinghouse in Venezuela for information on popular groups. One of its projects around that time was the compilation of a database containing information on community groups and their leaders. It was known that, in other countries, this type of information sometimes became the basis for death lists when it fell into inappropriate hands. Eventually Maryknoll cut all ties with CESAP.

In January 2004 the Coordinadora Democrática, whose only purpose was to oust Chávez, listed 27 political groups and 38 "nongovernmental organizations" as its membership—a very questionable role for NGOs.

The blame for the misuse of the term NGO should probably be placed on the local mass media. It was they who accepted its usage without clarification and who gave NGO's throughout the world a bad name in Venezuela, where no one thought of Boy Scouts or Girl Scouts when someone spoke of an NGO.

But there should be no excuse for the international media that continued the use of NGO outside of the country. "ADO" would have been a more appropriate term: Anti-Democratic Organizations. Actually, the international press could have included themselves in that category.

Stars, More or Less

A few weeks before the April coup, I asked a Venezuelan friend if he thought the same thing could occur in Venezuela that had happened in Chile on September 11, 1973, when Salvador Allende was overthrown by the dictator, General Augusto Pinochet. He replied in the negative and gave two reasons.

First, Allende had been elected president with only about one-third of the votes. Chávez had received almost 60 percent. Secondly, Allende did not have much support among the military. Chávez did.

As things turned out, the young man had identified the two reasons the coup in Venezuela failed.

On February 27, 1999, just a few weeks after he had assumed the presidency, Chávez sent federal troops into the barrios. Ten years before that date, Carlos Andrés Pérez had also considered doing the same thing. He did so the next day, and hundreds were killed.

But this time the troops were sent to repair school buildings, to help clean up neighborhoods, and to offer medical attention. Most of the young soldiers identified with the people in the barrios and the people with them. But some high-ranking officers did not see this as an appropriate task for the military. While it was common for soldiers to clean the yards around officers' houses, cleaning barrios was a different matter.

But Chávez's dream was an armed force similar to the kind Simón Bolívar wanted, an armed force of the people and with the people.

In time, there were accusations of corruption in the Plan Bolívar 2000, which was meant to be a collaborative effort of the armed forces and the civilian population. One of the generals in charge of the plan, who had been accused of corruption, later participated in the April 2002 coup.

Chávez had placed many military officers in civilian

leadership positions within the government. He erred in the confidence he placed in some, but many remained loyal to him. The same was true of those who remained within the ranks of the military.

He also had respect among the enlisted. This was especially evident in the "Casa Militar," the group of soldiers who guard the presidential palace and who accompany the president. Their rejoicing when Chávez returned from Orchila Island was recorded by photographers and television camera people. There was no doubt about their opinion of the coup.

So while the media rejoiced any time a high-ranking officer defected, my friend's analysis of the situation was correct: Chávez did have strong support within the military.

The Embassy

There is an old joke in Latin America that goes like this: "Do you know why there have never been any coup attempts in the United States? Simple. There is no U.S. embassy there."

A year after the coup, General Melvin López Hidalgo, the director of the Venezuelan National Security Board, said that he had proof that the United States was involved in it, and that he would make the evidence available at an appropriate moment. John Law, press attaché of the U.S. Embassy in Caracas, rejected the accusations.[33]

No one has yet shown that the United States government was directly involved in the attempted coup of April 2002 in Venezuela. But it was no secret that the U.S. government would have been happy to see Chávez out of power.

Even before his election, the U.S. government did not look favorably on him. In the 1998 campaign, while other candidates were able to travel to the United States to meet with people and to raise funds, the Clinton administration denied Chávez a visa. This was supposedly because he had led the attempted coup in 1992. However, when Carmona went into exile in Colombia after the 2002 coup, he was permitted to enter the U.S. and meet with people and give public presentations. The double standard was clear.

Sometimes the signals were subtle. As was mentioned before, Chávez often criticized the Venezuelan press for their partiality. One evening there was a small demonstration in front of the offices of *El Nacional*. Supporters of the government were tired of the newspaper's one-sided reporting and were protesting. The next day Donna Hrinak, the U.S. ambassador, visited the newspaper to express her support for freedom of the press. Such action would certainly be considered inappropriate if a foreign ambassador in the United States were to do the same. Statements by Colin Powell and the CIA to the Senate Foreign Relations Committee gave added support to the opposition.

As I have already mentioned, on my way to Austria in April 2002, I stopped in the United States. Daily we had seen photos of the constant flow of opposition members to and from the United States after meeting with government officials. I felt obligated to do what I could to try to offset, in some way, the lopsided negative messages they were carrying north about the Chávez government.

I decided to make an effort to meet with my senators and representative. I have often said that Wyomingites are politically the most powerful citizens in the United States. There are fewer than half a million people in Wyoming, and yet we have two senators and a congressman. About ten days before the coup, I was able to get an appointment with Senator Craig Thomas. His administrative assistant apologized because he could spare only about twenty minutes. I wondered how many people in New York can get that amount of time with one of their senators.

At the end of the visit, I gave Senator Thomas a written summary of the ideas I had presented, in which I included the following:

> "It is in the best interests of the United States that we foster friendly relations with the current Venezuelan government and that Chávez complete his term of presidency."

I concluded by saying that it was important that the United States government "maintain a position in favor of the democratic process in Venezuela and be clear about it." I added these two paragraphs also:

> "Much of the opposition to Chávez is composed of those who have benefited through the years from the rampant corruption and favoritism of previous governments. Everyone knows that little of the Venezuelan wealth has

trickled down to the ordinary person. Any support by the U.S. for the opposition looks like support for corruption. "Be careful about listening to opposition 'spokespersons.' In recent massive demonstrations, there have been no speakers. I think this is because the opposition cannot agree on who will speak. There seems to be a lot of jockeying for power. Dislike of Chávez is the only rallying point, but no leader has surfaced to fill the vacuum if he should be ousted and I think the possibility of a happy coalition government is impossible."

What the senator thought of what I said, I have no idea. But when the coup happened a few days later, the United States's response was quite contrary to my suggestions. Bart Jones, in an article that appeared in the *National Catholic Reporter,* May 3, 2002, summed it up nicely:

" The Bush administration not only did not condemn the April 12 coup, but appeared to endorse it and even blamed Chávez for his own downfall. 'Undemocratic actions committed or encouraged by the Chávez administration provoked yesterday's crisis in Venezuela,' the State Department said.

"After Chávez returned to power, National Security Adviser Condoleezza Rice warned not the coup leaders but, remarkably, Chávez to 'respect constitutional processes'."

The morning of the coup, Charles Shapiro, the United States ambassador in Caracas, went to the presidential palace and visited with the dictator Carmona. According to *The New York Times:* "Otto Reich, the under-secretary of state for Latin American affairs and a former United States ambassador to Venezuela... is believed to have called Mr. [Gustavo] Cisneros several times during the frenetic 48 hours

when Mr. Chávez was out of power to discuss the situation."
Mr. Cisneros was later accused by Chávez of being one of
the leaders of the coup.

Was the United States government involved in the coup?
Again, we may never know. Was the government happy? The
price of oil on the world market fell that day.

More Money

In addition to considering the involvement of the United States government, attention should also be given to the extent to which private companies in the United States assisted opposition efforts during the period of the April 2002 coup and in the months following.

As I have already mentioned, the Coca-Cola and Pepsi-Cola bottling plants did not function for almost two months at the end of 2002 and the beginning of 2003. While it is true that both companies had Venezuelan owners, do the mother companies lose complete control over what happens in the production of their product when they agree on a contract? That question will have to be asked in regard to each of the three situations that I will describe.

Bell South

Within hours after Carmona proclaimed himself president on April 12, an ad was prepared (or maybe it had been prepared beforehand), sponsored by Bell South and its Venezuelan affiliate, Telcel, giving its customers free long distance telephone calls to celebrate the overthrow of the government.

There were very few advertisements in the Caracas daily, *El Universal*, on April 13. But on page 3 of the second section there was a full-page ad with the following text:

"TELCEL celebrates with all of Venezuela FREEDOM. FREEDOM to call wherever you want, Long Distance Nationally, FREE from your Cellular or TELCELFIJO to whatever telephone, of whatever company, to celebrate with your loved ones the brilliant future that awaits us.
"TELCEL – BELLSOUTH"

There are many questions that should be asked about this ad:

Why did Bell South sponsor such an ad?
How is it possible that it was prepared so quickly?
Who authorized the ad?
Who authorized giving FREE long distance calls?
Why would a United States-based international company become involved in the internal affairs of another country?
Were U.S. stockholders informed of this action?
Did such action violate any U.S. laws?

I cannot answer any of these questions, but it would seem that someone at Bell South should. Personally, as a U.S. citizen living in Venezuela and as someone who feels strongly about democracy, I found Bell South's sponsorship of this ad offensive.

I came across the advertisement one day when I was going through old newspapers in the National Library. I was shocked. At the same time, there is a funny side to this story.

The Telcel-Bell South ad offered free long distance calls on April 14, not April 13. That was a mistake! By April 14 Chávez was back in power! Those who were celebrating that day were supporters of the legitimate government and not the coup leaders that Bell South and Telcel supported!

Wow! It was a perfect example of poetic justice. Shakespeare would have loved it! He probably could have developed a whole play from the scenario.

The Fast Food Franchises

Six days before Christmas 2002, in the middle of the indefinite "strike," I dropped down along the Venezuelan coast near Caracas. The Chinese restaurant was open. So was the restaurant owned by a Portuguese and another one owned by an Arab. The local pizzerias were also open. As a matter of fact, all the restaurants in the area were open. One exception: McDonald's was closed.

The forty or fifty stores in the shopping center were open. Subway, in the same shopping center, was closed.

The locally owned supermarkets and bakeries were all open. The gasoline stations were, too. Wendy's, in that same neighborhood, was not.

A good part of Caracas was alive and well that day. In Artigas, on Avenida San Martín, there was lots of activity, except at Kentucky Fried Chicken. It was closed. The same was true in other parts of the city: Burger King, Domino's Pizza, and Pizza Hut all had their lights off and their doors locked. They were joined in their "strike" by other Venezuelan food franchises, but the U.S.-based ones are the big ones.

My question was: who was on strike in Venezuela?

Surprisingly, very little physical damage was done to the closed establishments. Some had graffiti on them with expressions such as "Viva La Arepa" (Long Live the *Arepa*— a Venezuelan sandwich made with a cornmeal bread), but other than that, nothing much happened.

It might have been a blessing for the Venezuelans that so many fast-food restaurants were closed. Venezuelan food is delicious, and it is a tragedy that some are beginning to become addicted to what is called junk food in the United States. But, as an American citizen, I felt ashamed of what I was witnessing.

Mail Boxes Etc.

I had an account with Mail Boxes Etc. for several years, with personal mailboxes in Miami and Caracas. But after December 2, 2002, I wasn't able to receive my mail. I passed by their office several times, but the doors were locked, the

"CLOSED" sign displayed in the window, and no information as to how I could get my mail or voice a complaint was available.

Then, at the end of January, I received a call telling me that I could pick up my mail of the past two months. (For this I was paying about $20,00 for each two pounds.) However, the door would still be locked, the "CLOSED" sign would still appear in the window, and the lights inside the establishment would not be on. I was simply to knock on the door, someone would come to answer, and I could pick up my mail.

The reason? They were afraid that they would be seen as breaking the "strike" which the Coordinadora Democrática had imposed on them. Talk about fear! They were not afraid of any Bolivarian Circles. The Bolivarian Circles never touched their place of business. It was in exactly the same condition as when they had left it December 2. They were afraid of people like Carlos Ortega and Carlos Fernández.

I went and picked up my mail. There I found Christmas cards that Mail Boxes Etc. had received on December 4, December 5, December 6, etc. I now understood the reason for the "Etc." of Mail Boxes Etc. There were even some personal letters that I had sent to Susana from the United States in November. She didn't have to read them herself because I was already back in Venezuela from a speaking engagement. I could read them to her.

But this incident with Mail Boxes Etc. raised another question in my mind. What was happening at 2:00 a.m. when the Coordinadora Democrática and their henchmen were sleeping? Was it possible that McDonald's, Wendy's, Burger King, Pizza Hut, Domino's, KFC, Subway, and all the other U.S.-based food franchises were secretly opening their doors to those who had become addicted to their junk food?

Soon after, I terminated my contract with Mail Boxes Etc. I did this as soon as I felt they had delivered most of the mail they had hidden from me for a couple of months. The local owner and his employees were extremely nice, and I felt a friendship with them. But the people at the local post office were also friendly. The local post office's services are usually not as fast as that of Mail Boxes Etc., but at least I never had to sneak into the post office for fear that someone was going to look down on me for picking up my mail.

The Flag

When I was a child, we played a game called "Capture the Flag." The objective was to infiltrate the side of the opposition, grab their flag, and return to your own side untouched.

In Venezuela there is only one flag, but in 2002 the government opposition successfully made it their flag. A simple comparison of the massive demonstrations by the two sides will show that the opposition marches were overwhelmingly red, yellow, and blue. They had more flags. They had bigger flags. They had more flag-colored paraphernalia.

It started out in the early marches by groups of people carrying extremely large flags, approximately six yards by ten yards. They would be comparable to the flags flown in front of some restaurants in the United States to attract the attention of passersby. No one person could carry these flags. Thirty or forty persons would surround them, each grabbing an edge.

In some marches the advantage was twofold. One, such flags occupied a lot of space and helped to make the demonstration appear larger. Secondly, they made great media shots. An aerial view was definitely impressive.

Very rapidly, flags became hot items in the opposition marches, and if you saw someone on the subway carrying a flag, you knew they belonged to the opposition. How could one group of citizens claim the flag as their own? Money. The participants in the opposition marches simply had more money to buy such items, and one of the principal manufacturers of the flags was a member of the opposition.

The excessive use of the flag caused one young barrio woman to tell me: "I never thought I would see the day that I would cringe whenever I saw the flag of my country."

But government supporters also carried flags in their demonstrations, generally tiny ones, often made of paper. The constitution became the predominant symbol of the government supporters. However, the most popular edition of the constitution was that tiny blue book, about two by three inches! In the government marches, one would often see citizens holding the book high above their heads. Nice, but virtually unseen in any aerial shot.

In addition to the flag, the opposition stole slogans from the government supporters. A favorite one was "Prohibido Olvidar" (It is forbidden to forget.) In Venezuela, the words became prominent in 1990 on a poster to commemorate the victims of the February 27, 1989, massacre by government police forces. Yes, it was prohibited to forget these deaths, but they were forgotten in many ways. The barrio folk who had lost loved ones remembered them, but the annual commemoration of the date slipped into obscurity.

The opposition grabbed these words to draw attention to the few opposition people who had been killed in the April 11, 2002 demonstration that led up to the kidnapping and brief overthrow of Chávez. There were many more government supporters killed by police forces that day and the days following, but these were overlooked. As one opposition person told me, "The police had the right to kill them."

When Carlos Ortega was hiding in the Costa Rican embassy, waiting for his moment to leave the country, Acción Democrática named him honorary president of their party, and they appeared in front of the embassy with a huge flag. It bore the shield of the party and the words "Prohibido Olvidar." Acción Democrática controlled the country when the February 27 massacre took place! Feeling no shame for what they had caused in 1989, they were using words that had been meant to impugn *them*.

Another popular opposition phrase was "Ni un paso atrás" (Not one step back). This is the motto of Las Madres de La Plaza de Mayo in Argentina, a group the opposition would want no association with. But the motto? It now belonged to the opposition in Venezuela.

When flags of the Mothers of the Plaza de Mayo were carried in pro-government demonstrations, onlookers often looked confused. Wasn't that motto the property of the opposition?

In addition to the slogans, there were simply words that were given an opposition identity. Chávez was "an assassin" because of the April 11, 2002, deaths. Snipers opened fire on the people during the opposition demonstration, and the Metropolitan Police who were serving as escorts or bodyguards for the opposition also killed many people. But the opposition claimed that Chávez put the snipers there, a ridiculous and unfounded assertion. Ridiculous because if the government had put sharpshooters there, they would have attempted to kill opposition leaders and not innocent people. Unfounded because the government had nothing to gain from such deaths, and did not gain anything from them. The opposition used the deaths to start a coup and was the only sector that benefited from them. This would make *them* "the assassins," but they managed to label Chávez and his supporters with that tag.

Chávez was also called "a dictator." In all my years in Venezuela, there had never been more freedom. The only political prisoners were a few government supporters whom some judges managed to keep incarcerated for almost a year. When Carmona was detained, he was placed under house arrest. The same was true for Carlos Fernandez of FEDECAMARAS. Carmona, yes, had truly been a dictator, but the opposition never referred to him as such.

The opposition called themselves members of "the civil society" and their organizations were "civil associations." This was to distinguish themselves from the barrio people who were called "lumpen" and "hordes," among other demeaning names, and their organizations became "circles of terror."

When the opposition tried to join forces after the April 2002 coup, their organization was called the Coordinadora Democrática (the Democratic Coordination). Yet there was very little that was democratic about the organization. Who had elected their members? They were a part of the organization only because they wanted Chávez out. That was their only common purpose. Finding a way to get rid of a person whose supporters had won six elections doesn't sound particularly like an exercise in democracy.

The manipulation of words was so apparent that one writer compared the situation in Venezuela to George Orwell's *1984* where lies were truth and truth was lies. [34]

Conversations after the Performance

A Love (and Hate) Story

One day a Guajiro friend asked me, "Have you ever been in a country where the people loved their president as much as we do?" The question caught me off guard. I had never thought of anyone loving his or her president. Presidents are usually the lesser of two (or more) evils. They are the presidents because they got more votes than the other candidates. That's about it. Love? For a president?

His question made me think of another Venezuelan. He was sitting next to me on a flight between Barcelona (Venezuela) and Caracas. He had been reading some articles in *El Universal* about the October 10, 2002, antigovernment demonstration. I asked him what he thought about the marches that had been so common in Venezuela since December of 2001. I don't recall his exact response. I only know that I sensed a profound hatred, not love, for President Chávez.

So my friend's question became a twofold one for me: had I ever been in any country where the people not only so loved but also so hated their president?

Through the years I have been in all the Spanish- and Portuguese-speaking Central and South American countries except Honduras. I had to say to my friend, no, I couldn't think of any other country with feelings so intense. I was not saying that there weren't any. When I was in southern Brazil in 1989, I felt many people had a similar affection for Lula, but that was before he was president. And a foreign reporter told me that the people in Cuba love Fidel Castro. I have never been there.

But just as I couldn't think of any people outside of Venezuela loving their president, neither could I think of a country where I had sensed such an intense hatred for a president.

I have come to the conclusion that the situation that has existed in Venezuela in recent years has as much to do with love and hate as it does with politics and economics. And the love and hate goes all the way back to Chávez's rebellion on February 4, 1992. While he did have some support among the middle and upper classes, his strength was among the lower economic groups.

On that occasion, Chávez was to many people a Robin Hood or, in Latin American terms, a Zorro. He was a hero, struggling to take power away from those who had robbed and mistreated the working Venezuelan for decades.

I recall one day when I was in the home of an upper-middle-class family. The son was about forty years old and had not worked in over two years. He was looking for a job worthy of his talents, which seemed to be something in the executive category.

It was about ten or eleven in the morning when he came down in his bathrobe to eat breakfast. For some reason, much of his conversation seemed to be about the lazy people who lived in the barrios. There was a servant-woman scrubbing the floor. Another was cooking and serving him his breakfast. I knew that the family often insisted that these women be in their home until seven or eight at night, after which they would have to travel a distance to be with their own families. There were no whips, no chains, no electric shocks, but the place must have been a torture chamber for those women. Possibly "torture" is too strong a word. Maybe "twentieth-century slavery" would be a gentler way of describing it. Personally, I would have been inclined to hit the young man over the head with a frying pan if I had been one of those servants.

It is not hard to understand why, to people like these servant-women, Chávez was a hero. But to many others Chávez had disrupted the establishment and was a threat to anyone who had power. If he had succeeded in overthrowing President Carlos Andrés Pérez in 1992, what societal or political structure would have come next?

For the twentieth-century Venezuelan slaves, there was

immediate love and hope. Chávez's words, "Por ahora" (for now), were like Zorro's "Z." He would be back. For the slave masters there was immediate hate and concern that he might return. He did. And in spite of the fact that the commercial mass media would later say that everyone looked forward to a new era in Venezuela the day that Chávez was elected in 1998 with almost sixty percent of the votes, that was not true. About forty percent of the voters did not cast their ballots for Chávez and it was a dirty election as I have already indicated. No, everyone didn't look forward to a new day.

If we recognize love and hate as part of the problem we are dealing with, we can understand why dialog has been so difficult. Venezuela has been dealing with emotions, and these muddle matters.

Why do people love Chávez? I would center on one principal cause: they identify with him.

Why do people hate Chávez? I would name two basic reasons: one, racism; and, two, Venezuela's long history of corruption, political favoritism, and the abuse of the working class.

IDENTIFICATION

I was speaking to a seventy-year-old gardener one day and I asked him why he would vote for Chávez if elections were held again. His response: "He is like my grandson." Then he said, "He *is* my grandson."

Another day, a security guard at a private school told me, "I don't know what it is, but when Chávez speaks, I identify with what he is saying. He says things which I have felt for a long time."

When I was giving a ride to a middle-aged woman, she remarked: "Frankly, I have never been able to understand anything the presidents in Venezuela have said. My mother used to say that President Caldera was like a boiling pot of water: blurb, blurb, blurb. But this president is different. He uses language that I can understand."

Chávez seems to give the ordinary Venezuelan the feeling that he lives in their neighborhood, that he is a close relative, that he is accessible. When a working-class person calls him on the phone during his *Aló Presidente* program, you have the feeling that maybe someday he will take *your* call too. When he passes through the crowds on the back of a truck—that's the way barrio folks sometimes go to the cemetery to bury their neighbors—you sense that you could almost touch him, ride along with him, or have him ride along with you and your neighbors.

When he began his campaign for the presidency in the mid '90s, he traveled around the country and had personal contact with the people. He often sat in the audience at public gatherings and not on the speaker's stand.

When I ask people, "What has Chávez accomplished?" they often respond, "He has taken an interest in the little person." Usually when I ask them if he has helped them in some direct way the answer is, "no." But such ordinary people give me the feeling that they don't need his help; or, if they do, that someday he might help them, too.

One man answered: "Yes. I got a thousand-dollar loan with which I have been able to start a small business in my home. I was given three months without a payment to get it started, and I have to pay the rest back in two years. I've been able to keep up the payments so far. No government ever placed that kind of confidence in me before."

Another man said, "My father now gets his social security check each month and, according to the constitution, it has to be at least the minimum wage. That never happened before."

I asked a senior citizen what it was like trying to get his monthly check before Chávez's presidency. He mimicked carrying a cross on his shoulders. "That's what it was like," he said.

Other people talked about the 49 laws that Chávez enacted in November 2001. The new laws help the small fishing and business people. They made land available to the ordinary person.

Not all Venezuelans saw Chávez's actions so positively. I was on a bus one day when a caravan passed going in the other direction with Chávez on the back of a truck, waving to the people. A woman stood up, said she had lived in Venezuela for over twenty years and thought it was horrible the way the president acted. "What a disgrace: a president who sings when he is addressing the nation! Whoever heard of such a thing!" But barrio dwellers sang along with him.

When 500 Cuban doctors came to work in the barrios, opposition leaders complained because they were from Cuba. But the people in the barrios were glad to have doctors who not only attended to their needs, but lived in their homes and not in luxury apartments in the center of the city or in the suburbs, doctors who were in their makeshift consulting rooms in the mornings and visiting homes in the afternoons.

The literacy program also evoked repugnance from the opposition because it had been developed in Cuba. Even though it had gained worldwide recognition, it didn't matter. But people whose parents and grandparents as well as their grown children learned to read and write saw it differently.

A cab driver told me he was stuck in traffic one day when he overheard the conversation of two well-dressed men who were passing by. One was questioning the value of teaching a seventy-year-old person to read. The driver said to me, "Imagine what it would mean to a person to read the word 'airport' on that sign overhead for the first time in their life. What stupidity to say that teaching the elderly to read is of no importance. What a lack of sensitivity."

That ability to read has also made the new constitution available to the elderly, who hold it not only in their hands but close to their hearts.

Why do people love Chávez? Because he seems to care,

and because the programs the government is implementing reflect this, even if they don't touch everyone.

When I asked Susana why she went to Puente Llaguno that April day in 2002, she said she didn't go there because of Chávez. She went there because of the children and the future children of Venezuela.

I suppose the members of the opposition would answer the same way if they were asked why they are against Chávez. But while the ordinary person is looking only for decent health care, basic housing, and a good education, some of the opposition seem to be worried about their luxury cars, fancy homes, and the ability to send their children to universities outside the country. Both groups are talking about rights. Only the first is talking about basic ones.

RACISM

One day I picked up a copy of *USA TODAY* with a full-page advertisement showing a man who appeared to be an executive entering a Sheraton Hotel. His suit fit perfectly. The cuffs of his white shirt protruded subtly from the sleeves. His tie was radiant. He held a newspaper in his hands. His face was dominated by a smile. He seemed self-assured, relaxed. He was on his way to the top if he was not already there.

He was black.

I thought back to a different world, the world of Sesame Street. I remembered the children playing in the streets of New York, the animals living in trash cans, the classical and rock music mixed with laughter and smiles, the ordinary people doing ordinary things.

The children might have been black or white or brown or yellow or green. Color was not important.

But these were examples from the United States. Yes,

there is prejudice in the U.S. Everyone knows that, and most will admit it. But, somehow, I like to feel that there is a serious effort to get rid of it. That ad, those Sesame Street programs said that to me.

There has also been prejudice in Venezuela for ages, but no one talks about it. If they do, they deny it.

There are no well-known black commentators on Venezuelan television. There have been no black Miss Venezuelas. The major beer commercials present an almost naked blond.

A series of videocassettes (*Juana la Iguana*) was produced for children by a private firm to teach the songs and customs of Venezuela. The child protagonists are all upper-middle class. In one program, they go to their grandfather's farm where there is a servant-woman who works in the house—a far different world from that of Sesame Street.

One afternoon, almost a year after the coup, I was in the Mexico City airport awaiting a flight to Caracas. A middle-aged woman came and sat a few seats from me. I could tell she was agitated and seemed to want to talk to someone. Apparently fearing that I was a non-Spanish-speaking gringo, she turned and said to three men behind us, "None of you are Chavistas, right?"

One of the men laughed and jokingly said, "Sure, we all are."

She replied, "No, you can't be. You don't look like Chavistas."

With that, she entered into a prolonged conversation with all the other passengers near her—totally against the Chávez government and the "scum" that supported him. I just listened, fearful of saying anything because there had been disturbances on airplanes when members of the opposition recognized government figures. They would beat on their tray-tables and make the flight unbearable for the person, while rejoicing in their hermetically sealed power, 32,000 feet above sea level. A few pilots had landed their planes because of such disturbances. Venezuelan airports were probably the only ones in the world that had to put up warning signs saying that beating on tray-tables would not be tolerated.

I was not a public figure, and I didn't expect any tray-table beating, but I didn't want to be inside a plane for more than five hours in an unfriendly environment just because of some question I might raise.

Throughout the entire flight, however, I regretted that I had not asked her, "What does a Chavista look like?" My opportunity came when we landed and were waiting in line to go through immigration. The gods seemed to be helping me because this woman ended up directly behind me in the line of over one hundred people.

As our moment to be checked was nearing, I turned to her and said in Spanish, "Pardon me. I heard you saying to some gentlemen in the airport that they didn't look like Chavistas. Could you tell me what a Chavista looks like?" She replied immediately, "If you are fair-skinned and well educated, you are not a Chavista."

"Are there any Chavistas in line here?" I asked.

She looked at the still long line and replied, "No."

Yes, there is prejudice, although a middle-class friend told me that it was based on economics rather than skin color. He said, "If a black man has money, he can go wherever he wants and is welcome." That may be true. What he failed to recognize is how hard it is for a black man to ever get money.

What does this have to do with the present political situation in Venezuela? Chávez is not black, but he is dark brown. And at the root of the hatred for Chávez, skin color is one of the major factors.

The opposition demonstrations were often massive, with possibly hundreds of thousands present. There were scenes with token dark-skinned people who expressed their repudiation of Chávez, but the marchers were predominately white. Those who were there were better dressed, better educated, and earning more money than the dark-skinned Venezuelans who predominated in the marches in support of the government. Why?

There's no prejudice in Venezuela? You bet there is! It is part of the reason there is both love and hate for Chávez. And unless this factor is recognized and dealt with, no long-term peace is going to be possible in Venezuela.

ABUSE OF THE VENEZUELAN WORKING CLASS

In addition to the hate that President Chávez has provoked because of the color of his skin, there is a second matter that should be mentioned. It lies in what he says on behalf of the Venezuelan working class. His language is often blunt and might seem more appropriate in a military barracks or among a group of men playing dominoes. But it is not how he says things, although the commercial mass media would like to say that is the problem. It is simply what he says. His ideas are not pleasant to many ears.

Often what he says is a reflection of the songs of Alí Primera, songs the president sometimes sings during his Sunday program, *Aló Presidente*. The night he won the election in December 1998, loudspeakers blared Primera's songs.

As was mentioned previously, Alí Primera was a popular protest singer who died (or was killed) in a car accident in early 1985. His music was seldom heard on the radio, but walking through any barrio you could often hear his songs both played and sung.

The following will give you an example of the lyrics of his songs:

You are not going to believe this but there are schools here (in Venezuela) for dogs! where they teach the dogs not to leave teeth marks on their masters' newspapers. But their masters, for years and years, have been leaving teeth marks on their workers.

Those are the kinds of words that workers can appreciate when, after a hard day, they drag themselves home with a little bit of food for the family. They are not words that a factory owner would like to have played over the company intercom.

I know of a vice-president of a multinational firm who spent years hoping for his present position. He was often bypassed because, as his wife said, "He says what he believes, and bosses want to hear what they want to hear." Chávez has the same problem. He says what he thinks and what he believes. Such words are not always welcomed by everybody.

He often spoke of an "oligarchy" in Venezuela. The dictionary says this is a government in which power is in the hands of a few. The word describes what has been the Venezuelan reality for decades. In contrast, the promotion of small Bolívarian Circles, which tried to create the society that Simón Bolívar dreamt of, went directly contrary to the idea of oligarchy.

Venezuela was known for its corruption and with that must be included its abuse of the working class, against which the principal labor union (the CTV) did little.

Chávez's words have not been popular ones to those who benefited from these two cancers that Venezuela has suffered for so many years while the public was sold snake oil.

Chávez has had the terrible task of being like a doctor who brings bad news to a family. Venezuelan society is deathly ill and it has been for decades. It has been dominated by corrupt, self-seeking, financially motivated individuals, both Venezuelans and foreigners. A latent racism has been behind this domination.

You can try to kill the messenger if you want to do so, but the message will remain: Venezuela is deathly ill! The old order is dying, and that is why there is love and also hate for Chávez, not only in Venezuela but in other parts of the world as well.

Having said that, what comes to mind is the process people go through when they have a terminal disease. Those working with the dying speak of five phases: first, there is the shock and denial of reality when people learn they are going to die soon; second, there is anger which is often taken out on others; third there is a process of bargaining, even with God (I'll do this or that if...); fourth, depression comes, and then, finally, there is acceptance, peace. It should be noted that not all arrive at the final stage of acceptance and that a person may move back and forth between various phases.

I think Venezuela is going through a similar process. This is a society that had a façade of peacefulness and order—of good health. But there was widespread corruption and blatant brutality that took the lives of many people. Some of those lives were lost because of police action, others by the social neglect of politicians and business leaders who really didn't care what happened to the "little" people. Chávez's announcement that this world is dying has come as a shock to many.

First, there has been great denial. You can hear it frequently: "Everything was fine before; we were healthy" (and wealthy); "the poor were content in their own way;" "those who worked hard got paid well" (a lie). If we can get rid of Chávez, everything will be all right again. Kill the messenger. Yes, denial of the reality.

Secondly, there has been and there is anger. It is present in Venezuela; the air is thick with it. Just mention Chávez to many people and their faces tense up, and they take out their anger on you. A woman I had known for some time sat next to me on the bus one evening. She was friendly until I said something favorable about the government. Her face changed. She became angry—with me! Her hatred for Chávez (the messenger) was directed at me. That same anger was manifest during the coup when well-dressed people stormed the Cuban embassy because they thought Chávez might be there. Jumping on cars, breaking windows, cutting off the telephone and the electricity are not what members of the "civil society" are supposed to do.

Thirdly, there has also been a lot of bargaining, attempts to do anything rather than recognize that the old social order has to die. Marches, demonstrations, work stoppages, etc., give the feeling that death is being put off. You resort to bargaining with God. One evening there was a prayer vigil because the government declared security zones in certain parts of the city and prohibited demonstrations in these areas. Another day the commercial mass media, which had been the great defender of the ruling class, brought in a priest and minister to pray for peace when they gathered for a protest. On October 13, 2002, the day of the massive demonstration in support of the government, the opposition scheduled a Mass in the wealthy section of Caracas with musicians imported from Barlovento, a community known for its concentration of blacks.

And depression? The social scientists said that Venezuelans were having less sex because of the tension.

At some point, will Venezuela reach the stage of acceptance, of peace? That is the great unknown. But unless this stage is reached, it is going to be a terrible death for all involved. The patient who goes down hating the loving ones around the bed leaves a terrible memory.

On the other hand, if those who ruled for so long can accept that things have changed, that this death must come because a vile disease has infected the Venezuelan body for decades, maybe the country can move on.

One can only hope this will happen.

Love him or hate him, Chávez is not the problem. It is what he represents. An old and evil way of life is dying and those who enjoyed it so abundantly are fighting its death all the way.

Looking out of Different Windows

One day in 2003 I was leaving the airport in a taxi and driving along the coast. The young driver was not a fan of Chávez's government. His parents were from the Canary Islands, and he indicated that his papers were in order for him to move there soon.

As we drove, he commented repeatedly on all the failures of the government, including the lack of restoration efforts after the 1999 landslides. As I looked beyond him from the passenger's seat, I could see heavy equipment working on the restoration of the beaches. New sidewalks and decorative walls were being built. New trees and lampposts were being put in place. We passed over a new bridge under construction. He was the driver but often looked in my direction. He was seeing the mountains and the still-scarred landscape. I was the passenger and looked out the windows on his side of the vehicle. I was seeing progress.

We were both in the same automobile, but we were looking out of different windows.

In many ways that is what is happening in Venezuela. It is the story of the glass half full or half empty, depending on one's perspective.

A reporter with an international news service wrote me a letter in response to some of my editorials. He questioned why I didn't present the failures of the Chávez government in my writings. My response was that there didn't seem to be much need for that, in light of all the negative reporting that was being done. I also mentioned my negative experiences with previous governments and how I felt that much had changed since 1999.

What I have tried to present in this book is the perspective that a barrio person might have on the government: the failures of the government are overlooked. Is there still corruption? Sure. Are prices still high? Yes. Is it hard to get work? Too often.

But there are a million more children in school today than in 1998. Adults are learning to read and write. Public housing is light-years better than what it used to be. Senior citizens are receiving their monthly social security checks on time. There is health care that never existed before. Oil is bringing more money into the country. Chávez is responsible for these accomplishments.

Maybe I am looking out of only one window, but what I am seeing is real.

When upper-class readers of *El Universal* saw the picture of the woman seated on the curb with a sign reading, "Hungry and unemployed but I will stick with Chávez to the end," many might have laughed at the scene. But the hundreds of thousands of people who were also present were serious, and the smiles on their faces as they carried signs and chanted those words seemed to reflect what they truly felt.

Maybe they were hungry. Maybe they were unemployed. But they had hope. For some reason that was more important than anything else.

The Land of Giants

Once upon a time there was a country where many giants lived. Ordinary citizens greeted each other with a "hello," "good morning," "good afternoon" or whatever fit the occasion. The giants' greeting to one another was always the same: "Don't fall."

When my Mexican friend, Don Miguel Álvarez, told me that fable, he could see that I didn't get the point. He very kindly asked me, as though it was part of the story, "Do you know why they greeted each other that way?"

"No," I responded.

"The giants were so big they knew that if they ever fell they would never be able to get back up again."

I went to sleep that night pondering his words and woke up the next day with them imbedded in my mind. The story was about Venezuela.

I had been living in the land of the giants during the past few years.

First there were the generals and admirals who thought they were so important that they could claim a part of the city of Caracas as territory for their own battle. Time would show that officers without soldiers backing them are simply fake Mona Lisas, quickly removed from the museum when their lack of authenticity is discovered. They had their admirers...for a moment. One of the first to defect, Rear Admiral Carlos Molina Tamayo, left Venezuela for a self-imposed exile in El Salvador.

Then there was Pedro Carmona who, after rising to the presidency of the big business organization FEDECAMARAS, thought he could be president of the country. His conduct showed extreme insensitivity, a total lack of wisdom, even momentary insanity. In spite of the fact that other Latin American dictators had acted in similar ways in the past, this was Venezuela in 2002. Changing the name of a country and wiping out the constitution, the congress, and the supreme tribunal within hours after taking power was simply going too far. Eventually he fled to Colombia

Gradually, the triumvirate of the Coordinadora Democrática emerged: Carlos Ortega, Carlos Fernández, and Juan Fernández. As I write this, Carlos Fernández is in the United States for heart treatment; Carlos Ortega has gone into exile in Costa Rica; and Juan Fernández must have noticed at the rally on March 8, 2003, that there weren't the masses that used to be present when he and the others would mount the platform to speak. Even television coverage of the event that day wasn't what it used to be.

The triumvirate started a fight they thought they could win. They were wrong, and the damage they did is incalculable. Not only that: PDVSA is now going almost full speed again…with more than 15,000 fewer employees, most of them executives and office workers! One of their building complexes has been turned into a new public university.

To make matters even worse for the trio, the rest of the Coordinadora was happy about their absence. It gave them a chance to try to regroup. Among those who remain, there are still other giants. Will they also fall?

However, is the story of the giants really applicable to Venezuela? What about President Chávez? Shouldn't he be put in the giant category too? He fell. Why was he able to get up? Either the story is not valid or Chávez isn't a giant.

I like the second thesis and think it could be helpful in understanding what really has been happening in Venezuela.

Here's another story. In one part of the ocean there were some giant fish that were eating all the little ones. A few of the tiny creatures got together and decided they'd better think of something or they too would be eaten.

What they decided to do was to swim in formation so they would look like a big fish and thus scare their aggressors away. They did it, and it worked.

I would like to propose that Chávez is just a little fish,

not a giant one. He may not even be at the head of the movement. A woman said to me one day, "I'm not a follower of Chávez. Chávez is following my ideas!" Listening to Chávez on *Aló Presidente* I often hear him say to someone: "That's a great idea!"

Thus when Chávez was kidnapped, the organized fish didn't depend on him and didn't stop swimming. They turned around, tightened their ranks and because of their collective size, they scared the giant fish away, and Chávez, the little fish, was freed.

Those giants are going to try to come back. But the little fish have grown and the big fish haven't been eating as well as they used to. It is not going to be easy this time. Personally, I suggest that the big fish learn to make friends with the little fish. The little fish are willing.

Don't underestimate the importance of such an event, should it happen. A lot has transpired in the past few years. The blue Caribbean waters that touch Venezuela seem to be mingling with the Atlantic and Pacific oceans. It appears that some of them have already touched Brazil and Argentina. And Bolivia has always wanted to regain the access to the ocean that was taken away from her years ago by Chile.

If the big fish and little fish can learn to live together in Venezuela, the message might travel through all the waters of the world, and the world will be better for what Venezuela has suffered. Maybe even the giant fish in countries such as the United States, England, and Spain could learn from this lesson.

ANOTHER BEGINNING

Venezuela

One evening in September 2003 I was standing in a plaza in Queretaro, Mexico, in front of a statue in honor of Fray Junipero Serra, a Franciscan monk who worked in Mexico and founded missions all the way up the California coast to San Francisco. There was a plaque in front of the statue that read:

"To the great humanist, Fray Junípero Serra, who civilized the Pame and Jonace Peoples, an outstanding man who joined the Hispanic culture with the thousands of native cultures of the Sierra Gorda, where he left the profound mark of his dedication and solidarity with humanity.

"The people and government of Queretaro, dedicating this monument on the bicentenary of his death, also wish to honor the other heroic civilizers who shared with him in this imponderable accomplishment."

It all sounded so sweet and nice. How kind of these "humanists" to "civilize" a people who already had a culture and were already civilized before the Spaniards came to kill them and confiscate their property. For almost three hundred years before Serra's arrival, the Spaniards had been taking advantage of the native people. The people that Fray Junípero should have been civilizing were the Spaniards and not the natives.

The day after I stood in the plaza, I was facing not a statue but a live ninety-three–year-old man who lives in a shack about a half-hour from there, Don Andrés Vasquez de Santiago. I heard him tell how the priests taught him that his vocation in life was to work in the fields of the landowners and not to go to school. The priests also told the native people that they should not covet the property of the landowners since they had what they had because they had worked for it.

I wondered if there was a statue somewhere else in Mexico that praises the civilizing efforts of those priests as well.

In 1988, Pope John Paul II beatified Fray Junípero Serra, the last step before proclaiming him a "saint."

In 2003, President Chávez announced the beginning of some other missions. First there was *Misión Robinson,* an educational program attempting to wipe out illiteracy in Venezuela. Then came *Misión Ribas,* offering youth and adults the opportunity to finish high school, and *Misión Sucre,* making a college education available to thousands who had never been able to get through the doors of the existing public and private universities.

Misión Barrio Adentro sent doctors to live in the barrios and work among the people there. *Misión Guacaipuro* attempted to help the indigenous people in their struggles.

Sometimes those involved in these programs called themselves "missionaries." I would guess that this didn't sit well with some of the Catholic hierarchy and clergy who saw it as a bad use of a term belonging only to church activities. But considering their fundamental concepts, it is hard to see how anyone would criticize these efforts. Still there was heavy criticism by the opposition.

Remember the taxi driver who told me of hearing two well-dressed men saying that they saw no value in teaching elderly people how to read and write. There were others who said that the high school and college educations under the new programs would not be up to the usual standards.

But the biggest criticism was that they were bringing about the "Cubanization" of Venezuela. The literacy program had been developed in Cuba. The hundreds of doctors who moved into the barrios were mostly from Cuba. The books in a "Family Library," distributed to students throughout the country, were printed in Cuba.

It didn't matter that the literacy program had won recognition from the United Nations. It wasn't of importance that the Cuban doctors were doing what few Venezuelan doctors were willing to do. It wasn't noticed that the libraries contained books such as *Romeo and Juliet* by Shakespeare, *The Call of the Wild* by Jack London, *Cinderella,* and *Sleeping Beauty.* They were printed in Cuba and had to be bad.

Needless to say, the barrio people who were recipients of these programs saw things quite differently.

In February 2004 I accompanied some visitors from the United States on a tour of a couple of barrios. In one place a young man wanted to tell us what the "peaceful revolution" meant to him. He extended the palms of his hands out in front of him as though holding something precious, he told us that there were two bases for the process. One hand represented the *endógeno* dimension. The other, that of participatory democracy.

His use of the word *endógeno* threw me. I didn't know how to translate it. In spite of more than twenty years of formal education in the United States, I didn't know that the word endogenous existed, nor did I know its meaning. He explained to us that it meant that what was happening in Venezuela was coming from within the experience of the people. For centuries, he said, Latin America has had to live with economic, cultural, and social models imposed from outside. Now there was a search for new models that had meaning for the native population.

He then addressed the question of *participatory* democracy, which I have mentioned before, pointing out to the visitors the difference between simple representation and actual participation in the governing process.

All the visitors were impressed with the government activities they saw in the barrios. But a question lingered and overshadowed what they saw. Being related to the Catholic Church, they wondered why Chávez had been so critical of some of the hierarchy and why his relations with them had been so rocky.

Possibly most important of all was the question: was Chávez becoming too powerful?

That is a question difficult to answer when one is in the middle of a historical moment. Moses was a political figure as well as a religious one. He challenged the religious authorities and customs of his time; he also led the people out of Egypt. Is it possible that Chávez will some day be seen as another Moses? Or is it even possible that some Pope three hundred years from now will declare him a saint for founding the *"missions?"*

Who knows? But what seems more important to me is the realization that Chávez, and probably Moses, had their power because of the people they spoke for. They became megaphones for ideas and dreams existing within the ordinary person that had been repressed for too many years.

When Moses disappeared from the scene, his people did not. Someday Chávez will not be governing Venezuela, but I am convinced that the dreams he has given voice to will not die.

As I write the last paragraphs of this book, I am looking at a 1000-peso bill from Colombia. It bears the likeness of Jorge Eliécer Gaitán. Gaitán was a candidate for the presidency of Colombia when he was assassinated on April 9, 1948. He represented the hopes of the ordinary Colombian at the time. Today, many see his death as the beginning of the guerrilla movement in Colombia.

The bill carries a quotation from Gaitán, "I am not a man. I am a people." President Chávez repeated those words on April 13, 2003, the first anniversary of his return to the presidency.

I have no idea what the future of Hugo Chávez Frías will be. But this book is not meant to be a book about Hugo Chávez nor is it about a giant. It is about a process, a people, the common Venezuelan people—perhaps not only the best-kept secret of the Caribbean, but also the world's best-kept secret of democracy.

Endnotes

[1] I have since changed my mind about *The New York Times*. Their reporting about Venezuela was extremely biased and often presented a very distorted picture of what was happening—a far cry from my childhood opinion of the newspaper.

Justin Delacour, a doctoral student of political science at the University of New Mexico, discovered that between April 12, 2002, and October 12, 2004, the *Times* cited "independent" analysts unfavorable to the Venezuelan government forty-two times.

Those favorable were mentioned only six times.

[2] Barrio is a Spanish word that means "neighborhood." In Venezuela it is used to refer only to low-income neighborhoods. *Favela* would be the word used in Brazil. Unless otherwise noted, all translations are those of the author.

[3] *"Yip"* is a term used by barrio dwellers for the old Toyota Land Cruisers used for public transportation in the hillsides that surround Caracas. It is pronounced like "Jeep" in English. These vehicles could carry twelve people, two in front and ten squashed in the back on hard slabs of wood covered with a bit of padding.

[4] The Guajiros are one of many indigenous groups in Venezuela.

[5] *El día que bajaron los cerros*, Editorial Ateneo de Caracas, Caracas 1989, p. 13.

[6] Page 743.

[7] Page 169.

[8] PROVEA is an acronym for Programa Venezolano de Educación-Acción en Derechos Humanos, A Venezuelan Program of Education-Action in Human Rights.

[9] A satellite community of Caracas.

[10] Venezuela's third largest city, about two-and-a-half hours from Caracas.

[11] Situación de los Derechos Humanos en Venezuela, Informe Anual Octubre 1991 Septiembre 1992, p.iv

[12] When he did win, the value went up, not down for several months.

[13] MVR stands for the Movimiento Quinta República (the Movement toward the Fifth Republic).

[14] September 29, 2002

[15] Miraflores is about six miles from Chacao.

[16] Venezuela's Supreme Court.

[17] The Metropolitan Police are under the control of the Alcalde Mayor of Caracas, a role similar to that of the Mayor of New York City. The Alcalde Mayor of Caracas at the time, Alfredo Peña, was an outspoken critic of Chávez. He had switched to the opposition soon after he had been elected on Chávez' shirttails. The Metropolitan Police were used regularly to act as a protective shield for the opposition in their marches but were never seen at government demonstrations.

[18] A barrio of Caracas.

[19] *Perdigones* are metal and plastic pellets, buckshot. The Metropolitan Police killed a very good friend of Susana, Sergio Rodriquez, using perdigones against a student demonstration September 23, 1993.

[20] Fuerte Tiuna (Fort Tiuna) is the principal military base in Caracas.

[21] The Casa Militar houses the presidential guard.

[22] The red beret as well as the color red became a symbol of government supporters. The soldiers had changed their berets when Carmona took over as president.

[23] Susana's words: "At the same time, it has to be mentioned that there were people who were trying to take advantage of the situation by looting during these days. But credit has to be given to the Bolivarian Circles that there was not more looting. In our neighborhood only two grocery stores were looted because of the efforts of those who were in the Circles to prevent it. The looting started with the coup."

[24] Although Chávez had been the proponent and main supporter of the idea of a presidential referendum, the Associated Press release from Caracas said, "International pressure forced President Hugo Chávez to accept a likely recall referendum...."

[25] The exception: a young woman in the working-class neighborhood of the 23 de Enero, replied that a result unfavorable to the government would not be acceptable and that she would be willing to fight to see that Chávez would not be ousted from power.

[26] Readers outside of Latin America may not be aware of the growing movement among indigenous people demanding their recognition in society. The Zapatista movement in Mexico would be one manifestation of this. The political unrest in Bolivia is basically due to a lack of recognition of the Aymara and Quechua people, who are the majority of Bolivia's inhabitants.

[27] Simon Romero, "Coup? Not Cisneros's Style. But Power? Oh, Yes." *The New York Times*, 28 April 2002. I would recommend this article as a source for basic information on Gustavo Cisneros.

[28] I have relied on a small booklet by Guillermo García Ponce, *Chávez y la Batalla del Petróleo*, Editorial Fuentes, 2000, for much of the information about the history of oil in Venezuela.

[29] The question of "meritocracy" sounds very hollow to a barrio person. To be a petroleum executive, one needs a college education, something very difficult to obtain if you are not wealthy, a graduate of a private school, or someone with a lot of political pull.

[30] There was the election of Chávez in 1998. Then followed the referendum to have a constitutional congress, another election to decide who would be its members, and finally the referendum to approve the constitution. Then there was the election that re-elected Chávez under the new constitution, followed by the election of mayors and governors who heavily supported Chávez.

[31] There is an ecumenical group in Brazil called CESEP (with two "E's" in its acronym). It is in no way related to CESAP.

[32] Olive Branch Press, 2006.

[33] *Últimas Noticias*, April 16, 2003.

[34] Roberto Hernández Montoya, "La Inquisición Mediática," *Questión,* Julio 2002.

Currently residing in Venezuela, **Charles Hardy** has been writing and speaking about the political and social reality of Latin America for over forty years. Born in Wyoming, he has visited almost every Central and South American country, and, as a Catholic priest, lived eight years in a cardboard shack in a Venezuelan barrio. He has been a frequent contributor to www.narconews.com. His personal blog is www.cowboyincaracas.com.

James W. Russell is the Connecticut State University professor of Sociology and coordinator of Latin American Studies at Eastern Connecticut State University. He is the author of six books, including *Double Standard: Social Policy in Europe and the United States* (Rowman & Littlefield) and *After the Fifth Sun: Class and Race in North America* (Prentice Hall).

Curbstone Press, Inc.

is a non-profit publishing house dedicated to multicultural literature that reflects a commitment to social awareness and change, with an emphasis on contemporary writing from Latino, Latin American and Vietnamese cultures.

Curbstone's dual-pronged mission focuses on both publishing creative writers whose work promotes human rights and intercultural understanding, and on bringing these writers and the issues they illuminate into the community. Curbstone builds bridges between its writers and the public—from inner-city to rural areas, colleges to community centers, children to adults, with a particular interest in underfunded public schools. This involves enriching school curricula, reaching out to underserved audiences by donating books and conducting readings and community programs, and promoting discussion in the media. It is only through these combined efforts that literature can truly make a difference.

Curbstone Press, like all non-profit presses, relies heavily on the support of individuals, foundations, and government agencies to bring you, the reader, works of literary merit and social significance that would likely not find a place in profit-driven publishing channels, and to bring these authors and their books into communities across the country.

If you wish to become a supporter of a specific book—one that is already published or one that is about to be published—your contribution will support not only the book's publication but also its continuation through reprints.

We invite you to support Curbstone's efforts to present the diverse voices and views that make our culture richer. Tax-deductible donations can be made by check or credit card to:
Curbstone Press, 321 Jackson Street, Willimantic, CT 06226
phone: (860) 423-5110   fax: (860) 423-9242
www.curbstone.org